Understanding Your BABY's Sensory Signals

Keep it Real. Keep it Simple. Keep it Sensory.

Angie Voss, OTR

Copyright © 2014 Angie Voss, OTR

All rights reserved.

ASensoryLife.com

ISBN-13: 978-1496152480
ISBN-10: 1496152484

A Moment for Gratitude

It is with the utmost respect, honor, and love that I first and foremost offer gratitude to my Mom, my editor in chief, Bonnie Post. You are always behind the scenes, not only cheering me on and supporting me, but editing my work and providing me honest feedback anytime I need it. Not only that, as an incredibly gifted and experienced educator, you have changed the lives of so many children in your classrooms with the zest and passion for sensory tools and strategies in the schools. You have such a giving and loving spirit, no wonder I find these to be my greatest gifts and strengths.

P.S. I do hope this page is up to your grammatical standards, as it is a surprise and was added after your final editing. ☺

It is with a heart full of love that I would like to express gratitude to my dear friend Holly Carman and my little animal loving, buddy Meg Carman for allowing my use of this simply adorable and perfect photo for the cover of the book. I am forever grateful that our paths have crossed, and I look forward to sharing in the joy and delight of watching Meg grow up to be the perfect, beautiful, and talented girl that she is destined to be, with so very much to offer this world.

A special thanks to Kim Lowe, of Kim Lowe Photography (kimlowe.com) for the generous contribution of the cover photo. You are such a talented photographer and your love for your work and art shines through.

Dearest Lindsey Lieneck, OTR, we are indeed kindred OT spirits. Thank you for always encouraging me behind the scenes. You inspire me and you have played such a pivotal role in my life during these years of transition from a clinician in my private practice, to an author in our field. I look forward to our journey together for many years to come.

And last, but surely not least, Kathy Weinert, PT! You were the inspiration behind this book! I always knew I wanted to somehow reach out to the parents of our babies coming in to this world, I just wasn't sure how to best do it. Thank you for your brilliant idea and thank you for all you do for the little lives you touch as an amazing therapist.

Dear Reader:

It is my hope that as you read this book you will feel as though you're sitting with me at my kitchen table sharing a cup of coffee and talking about your precious, perfect new little bundle of love. To get that casual conversational feeling, I have taken grammatical liberties that would make my high school English teachers (and my editor) get out the red pen. The thing is . . . I write the way I talk...not in the informational textbook style. So if I don't have perfect subject/verb agreement or correct pronoun usage, please know that this is what works for me, and I hope it works for you, as well.

How to Use This Handbook

Table of Contents: The table of contents provides a list of the sensory signals discussed in the book.

Sensory Signal: The title of each page describes the sensory difference or preference ("signal") that a baby may be displaying. This signal is your cue that an adaptation, modification, or increase/decrease in sensory input is likely being indicated.

Ideas to Help: This handbook is intended to be user-friendly, so try not to overthink each item. If the sensory signal applies, dive right into the "Ideas to Help" section! The suggested ideas are beneficial to all babies and cannot be harmful in any way. You will find that many of the same suggestions are listed under more than one sensory signal. The best part about this is that you will then know that one sensory technique is benefiting more than one area of concern!

Early intervention is the key. Trust your gut. Trust your instincts.

If you find that your baby is giving you quite a few sensory signals, or so severe in nature that it is impacting overall development, quality of life, and interaction within the environment, an evaluation by a sensory based OT or PT is strongly recommended. Please don't let this frighten you, it is much easier and more effective to understand your baby's sensory needs and respond accordingly to possible sensory concerns now, rather than later. The brain has an enormous amount of neuroplasticity during the first 3 years of life. Sensory based intervention, along with daily application of sensory tools and strategies can help change and develop the sensory pathways in order for proper overall development.

Contents

Breast Feeds Well But Refuses Baby Food 7

Wants Constant Touching and Holding or None at All, Goes From One Extreme to the Other 8

One Moment Sensitive to Sound and the Next Moment Not Affected at All 9

Difficulty Going Outside in Wind and Rain, Very Upset and Crying 10

Very Slight Change in Environment Causes Screaming and Crying.........................11

Dislikes Cloth Diapers, Only Comfortable in Disposable Diapers.........................12

Loves to Be Turned Upside Down, Demands It.........................13

Likes to Spend Extensive Amounts of Time in the Crib 14

Very Demanding 15

Craves Movement but Is Easily Overstimulated.........................16

Excessive Difficulty with Teething.........................17

Dislikes Swaddling.........................18

Difficulty Learning to Sit Independently.........................19

Very Slow to Achieve Gross Motor Milestones such as Rolling, Crawling, or Walking 20

Frequent Sneezing 22

Excessive Sleeping (Shutdown) 23

Unusually Short Periods of Sleep 24

Dislikes Laying on Back.........................26

Constant Need for Thumb Sucking/Pacifier.........................27

Needs VERY Big Movements to Soothe and Calm (rocking, swinging, bouncing)..28

Turns Body and Head Away from Caregiver when Bottle Feeding 29

Needs Cheeks Stuffed Very Full to Chew and Swallow.........................30

Extreme Difficulty with Falling Asleep 31

Unable to Self-Soothe.........................32

Dislikes Being Touched and/or Held; Calms When Put Down.........................33

Prefers Being in the Dark When Awake 34

Head Being Tipped Backwards Is Not Tolerated Well 35

Will Only Breastfeed in the Dark 36

Excessive Bouncing, Including Bouncing on Bottom Across the Floor..................37

Dislikes Car Seats, Particularly Backward Facing 38

Dislikes Sleep Sacks and/or Pajamas with Feet 39

Constant Movement of Arms and Legs 40

Tensing Up or Shaking of the Hands 41

Dislikes Riding in the Car at Night 42

Dislikes Outfit Changes and Certain Clothing 43

Shuts Down in Social Situations Outside of the Home 44

Not Mouthing Objects...45

Limp/Floppy Body 46

Lacks Awareness of Body in Space and Body Position 47

Arches Back Often 48

Loud or Unexpected Sounds Are Startling or Cause Fear....................................49

Frequently Rubs Ears and Head..50

Loves to Get Messy and Engage in Full Body Messy Play 52

Always Holds a Special Object or Blanket 53

Best with Breastfeeding or a Bottle When Drowsy or Asleep 54

Stiffens Body or Arches during Breast or Bottle Feedings 55

Latches and Unlatches during Breast Feeding or Bottle Feeding...........................56

Searches Frantically When Trying to Latch for Breastfeeding 57

Needs Constant Swaddling to Stay Calm 58

Bath Time is Difficult 59

Body Feels Stiff and/or Stiffens Frequently 60

Avoids Crawling on All Fours and/or Prefers Scooting on the Bottom 61

Avoids Facing in When Held, Prefers Facing Outward 62

Does Not Like Kisses 63

Has to Be Held to Fall Asleep...64

Flushing of Cheeks 65

Enjoys Repetitive Play 66

Dislikes Hair Washing and Water Poured Over the Head.........................67

Loves to Be Naked 68

Holds Arms Up and Twists Hands in Circles...69

Shakes or Rolls Head 70

Does Not Seem to Get Hungry or Eats Way Too Much or Too Quickly.....71

Gets Sick or Nauseous After Swinging 72

Frequent Spitting Up 73

Licks Everything, Including People and Objects......................................74

Bites Self or Others 75

Sleeps Between Crib Mattress and Edge of Crib, Craves Tight Spaces 76

Refuses to Touch Grass or Sand 77

Approaches Play or New Textures with Closed Fists or Withdraws Hands ...78

Avoids Eye Contact or Shifts Gaze...79

Gags with Textured Foods, Picky Eater, Extreme Food Preferences 80

Nail Trimming Distress...81

Messy Play Is Distressing and Avoided, Including at Mealtime 82

Hiccups Frequently 83

Resists Movement Such as Swinging, Bouncing, Rocking.........................84

Touches Objects Very Lightly...85

Does Not Mouth Objects 86

Hair Brushing Distress...87

Prefers to "W" Sit...88

Dislikes Being Outside 89

Very Difficult to Calm 90

Dislikes Wearing Shoes and/or Socks...91

Loves to Look at Spinning or Shiny Objects 92

Smashes and Grinds Face into Stuffed Animals or Soft Objects (Usually Mouth Open) 93

Rubs Head Along Floor (Bull Dozing) 94

Glazed-Over Look in Eyes 95

Does Not Feel Pain Like Others, Seems to Lack Awareness of Pain 96

Overheats Very Easily/Poor Temperature Regulation 97

Loves to Be Wrapped Tightly in Blankets and Swaddled 98

Hair Pulling on Self 99

Scratches Self 100

Bangs Toys and Objects Excessively and Intensely 101

Seeks Vibration to Mouth 102

Drools Excessively 103

Breast Feeds Well But Refuses Baby Food

Sensory Explanation: A baby who breast feeds well but refuses baby food is likely not ready for the sensory experience and multi-sensory input presented by the food. Baby food involves new texture, smell, taste, temperature of the food and the texture presented by the spoon. One or more of the sensory systems may be over-registering information and needs more time to mature and process more efficiently.

Ideas to Help!

- **Do not force the issue. The more you force it, the longer it will take for the baby's sensory systems to be ready to accept the new sensory experience.**
- **Try various spoons with different textures and sizes.**
- **Encourage messy play and independent hand to mouth exploration of the baby food (simply place a spoonful on the tray and let the little one explore).**
- **There is no specific time frame in which a baby "should" accept the food texture…let it happen naturally. As long as the baby is breastfeeding well, he is getting the proper nutrition.**
- **Encourage mouthing and exploration with oral sensory tools throughout the day.**
- **Try a variety of "first foods", staying away from the baby cereals which provide very little nutritional value. Begin with fruits that are also sweet like breast milk, such as bananas, avocado, sweet potato, or yams. Stick to single ingredient foods.**
- **Do not begin baby food until at least 6 months of age, as this can decrease the risk of food allergies as well as allow for more maturity with the sensory systems.**

Wants Constant Touching and Holding or None at All, Goes From One Extreme to the Other

Sensory Explanation: This is most likely due to difficulty with sensory modulation. The nervous system and brain is not processing the sensory input efficiently and it creates a "traffic jam" in the brain; so even though the sensory input is tolerated and accepted one minute, the brain puts a halt to it so it can sort out and organize all of the input received. Another explanation may be a change in sensory input, such as going from deep pressure touch to light touch, or adding in movement or sound to the situation…all forms of sensory input must be considered. Infants can also quickly transition to needing sleep, which should also be considered as a possible factor at any given moment. The little one simply needs a break from all of the sensory input.

Ideas to Help!

- Be very aware of the type of tactile input you are providing. Deep pressure touch is generally tolerated more than light touch.
- Be aware of any other forms of sensory input which may be a factor at that moment, such as movement, sound, light, smells, etc…adjust and adapt.
- Respect this sensory signal and provide a quiet, low stimuli environment for the baby with calming and soothing input.
- Swaddling or wrapping tightly in a blanket may be helpful.
- Form-fitting, snug comfortable clothing can provide an ongoing dose of deep pressure touch which is regulating for the nervous system.
- Regular and frequent use of a baby carrier/sling (the soft body conforming type) is an excellent tool to support neurobehavioral organization.

One Moment Sensitive to Sound and the Next Moment Not Affected at All

Sensory Explanation: Sound comes in many forms: different tones, pitches, and frequencies. Sound also can be unexpected or of a gradual onset. The auditory system processes and accepts all different types independently. For example, you may be sensitive to the sound of styrofoam but fine with the sound of fingernails on a chalkboard. Another explanation for this sensory signal can be the state of regulation…if the baby is tired or simply has had enough sensory input, the nervous system may react to a certain sound that normally does not bother her.

Ideas to Help!

- Use this as a cue to decrease the amount of sensory input overall for the baby, providing a low-stimuli, calming and soothing environment.
- Be prepared with noise cancelling headphones for your little one (Baby Banz) for situations where sound may be overwhelming and uncomfortable.
- Assess the situation. Is the baby tired, hungry, and overstimulated? Adjust and respond.
- Providing a snug over the ears knit hat is a great way to decrease auditory input in all seasons and can help take the edge off when it comes to loud, unexpected, and harsh sounds.
- A hood is also a great way to decrease auditory input.

Difficulty Going Outside in Wind and Rain, Very Upset and Crying

Sensory Explanation: Wind and rain are forms of sensory input that can be painful and very uncomfortable to the tactile system, especially on the face. Wind and rain are both unpredictable, unexpected, and out of the ordinary forms of sensory input...especially for a baby. If the baby over-registers tactile input in general, this can be even more difficult for the baby's tactile system to process and accept. Keep in mind the very young tactile system is still learning to accept and process various types of tactile input, this applies to all babies.

Ideas to Help!

- Respect this sensory signal and be sure to cover the baby with a blanket anytime you go outside in the wind or rain. Every time. Otherwise the brain will begin to develop a negative pattern and memory of the possibly noxious and unpredictable input, triggering fight or flight without warning or at the slightest breeze.
- Try baby sunglasses and a bucket type hat, fisherman type hat, or a hood when outdoors as a starting point until the nervous system matures and develops.
- Try to always be prepared with these sensory tools for defensiveness, and refrain from the quick and frantic run from the car to the house carrying the baby...this can create even more sensory overload and overstimulation.
- You never know when wind or rain will start, so being proactive and on guard is key.

Very Slight Change in Environment Causes Screaming and Crying

Sensory Explanation: Every single form or sensory input can be a potential threat to the nervous system if a baby is having a difficult time processing information. The slightest change in light, sound, smell, touch, movement, etc. can trigger a sensory response of fight or flight and the nervous system being "on guard". Even the way the light may be shining in the window through the blinds can be painful for the baby. It is very important to respect the slightest amount of sensory input as very powerful.

Ideas to Help!

- **Acting as a sensory detective will be a key to your success in understanding the sensory triggers for your baby. Watch for every tiny change in the environment, as it can be the slightest amount of input that triggers dysregulation.**
- **Increase the amount of tactile input, particularly deep pressure touch to support self-regulation.**
- **Increase the amount of vestibular input using the planes (directions) of movement tolerated best...such as bouncing or swinging back and forth or side to side.**
- **Increase the amount of proprioceptive input via swaddling, a soft sling baby carrier, or a squish box, if age appropriate.**
- **Limit the amount of time spent in unfamiliar places until self-regulation improves.**
- **Focus on calm, quiet, familiar settings.**
- **Spending time outdoors in your own backyard is just as beneficial as going to the park.**

Dislikes Cloth Diapers, Only Comfortable in Disposable Diapers

Sensory Explanation: If a baby is having difficulty processing tactile input and over-registering the information, the difference between a cloth and disposable diaper is profound. Although I strongly encourage cloth diapers for the environmental and health aspect, sometimes it is just not feasible.

Ideas to Help!

- Use disposable diapers until the tactile system is mature enough and ready to accept the different type of diaper.
- Determine if it is the fit of the diaper that may be the problem. See if you can duplicate the fit of the cloth diaper with the disposable diaper.
- Assess the situation in regards to the fasteners with the cloth diaper to determine if that is the part bothering the baby. Simply as a trial…use strong tape to secure the diaper and see how the little one responds.
- Try different textures and brands of cloth diapers, the difference may be subtle to you but not to the over-responsive tactile system of the baby.
- Encourage full body messy play and other tactile based play. This will help the tactile system to develop overall.
- Provide regular and daily doses of full body deep pressure touch.

Loves to Be Turned Upside Down, Demands It

Sensory Explanation: Inverting the head, which is what is achieved when you turn your little one upside down, is an incredibly powerful form of vestibular input. Not only that, it provides a dose of joint traction to the neck and spine. Both of these forms of sensory input are regulating, organizing, and beneficial for brain and sensory development. And in the event that the youngster is under-registering sensory input via the vestibular and/or proprioceptive systems, they may crave being upside down because they can "feel it".

Ideas to Help!

- **Turn that lil' cutie upside down all he wants, just always be sure to return back to upright slowly and with caution.**
- **Use this as an indicator that an increase in vestibular input is needed.**
- **Focus on frequent and regular doses of swinging, bouncing, and rocking throughout the day.**
- **Use an exercise ball or peanut ball to provide head inversion.**
- **Increase the amount of proprioception throughout the day via lots of climbing, crawling, rolling, etc.**
- **Depending on the level of mobility, create safe mini obstacle courses in the home.**
- **Let the little one move, move, move!**

Likes to Spend Extensive Amounts of Time in the Crib

Sensory Explanation: If a baby is having a difficult time processing multi-sensory input, such as sound, movement, or touch, the crib may serve as a sensory retreat for the baby…providing a quiet, calm, low stimuli environment. Other factors which may come in to play are the familiar and predictable forms of sensory input found within the crib, such as a hanging mobile or the smell of the blankets, which may be very comforting and soothing to the nervous system.

Ideas to Help!

- **Respect this as a sensory need, knowing that it is helping with neurobehavioral organization and self-regulation.**
- **Decrease the sensory stimuli within the home to see if this helps the baby feel more comfortable within the environment outside of the crib.**
- **Use swaddling or a soft sling baby carrier throughout the day to help the nervous system to regulate and process information.**
- **With direct supervision, create a sensory retreat in the common area of the home, such as a squish box or the use of a memory foam beanbag.**

Very Demanding

Sensory Explanation: This is completely normal! Babies are supposed to be demanding. It is the time in development that bonding, nurturing, and attention are of the utmost importance. Contrary to popular belief, you will not spoil your child by giving the attention and love that they seek out when they are very young...you will help lay a strong foundation.

Ideas to Help!

- Little ones physically need as much attention as you can give them. Holding, cuddling, and showing affection gives the brain and nervous system essential sensory input and nutrition. This is the time in the baby's life that they need this sensory input the most.
- When you are interacting, get the most sensory bang for your buck by incorporating movement (vestibular input), proprioception, and deep pressure touch.
- Provide movement in various directions/planes, those which are tolerated well and enjoyed by the baby...such as bouncing, swaying side to side, being tipped upside down.
- Utilize a soft body conforming carrier for the times when you need to get things done and to provide the physical attention that the little one needs. Using a baby carrier provides vestibular input and full body deep pressure touch the entire time.

Craves Movement but Is Easily Overstimulated

Sensory Explanation: This is most likely a sign of difficulty with sensory modulation, primarily with processing of vestibular input. Vestibular input is very powerful and the nervous system may be having difficulty processing the input efficiently. Another explanation could be that the baby tolerates movement in one plane (direction), but not another. For example, perhaps you are bouncing the baby on your knee, and then switch direction to swaying side to side. The vestibular system processes each plane of movement separately.

Ideas to Help!

- Watch closely for the sensory signals and body language the baby gives you. The cues may be subtle but are significant in how to respond to incorporating and trying new types of movement. Even a slight change in facial expression or tensing of the hands can be a reaction to movement, so if it seems like he/she is getting overstimulated, then stop.
- Stop means stop when it comes to movement based activities in this situation. Follow up with full body deep pressure touch, swaddling, or some type of sensory retreat that will help the brain unload all of that powerful input.
- Stick to one plane/direction of movement at a time, allowing at least a 1 minute break between switching planes.
- Incorporating full body deep pressure touch and proprioception while swinging can help the nervous system process more efficiently. Examples include using a cuddle type swing or swinging in a blanket.
- Provide a large amount of vertical vestibular input, as it is typically the most tolerated plane of movement and can help the vestibular system develop overall. Examples include bouncing on your knee, bouncing the little one while seated on a therapy/exercise ball, or using bouncing type stationary toys.

Excessive Difficulty with Teething

Sensory Explanation: Your little one may be over-registering pain which is a component of the tactile system. On the other hand the gums and teeth may truly be having difficulty in cutting the teeth. Either the gums may be very thick, and/or the teeth may not be strong enough to push through. Nutrition plays a large role in strong teeth.

Ideas to Help!

- Try popsicles made out of breast milk or other healthy frozen liquid and place in a Munchkin mesh feeder which will prevent choking.
- Provide a vibrating type oral sensory tool.
- Use the mesh feeder for other cold or frozen foods such as a raw carrot, strawberries, or bananas.
- Deep pressure touch and massage to the cheeks and jaw can very soothing.
- Feed fresh, whole, raw organic foods with the proper nutritional content.

Dislikes Swaddling

Sensory Explanation: Typically full body deep pressure touch and proprioception are the most tolerated forms of sensory input for everyone, including those with sensory processing difficulties. With this said, it is important to closely assess the situation...for instance it may be the light touch of the blanket edge close to the face that is triggering the dislike for swaddling. Maybe the blanket is not being wrapped tightly enough, causing more light touch rather than deep pressure touch. Perhaps the little one does not tolerate full body flexion well, especially if we are talking about a premature baby. Full body flexion is not a familiar position for an infant born premature due to not reaching full term and the "squish factor" while inside the uterus.

Ideas to Help!

- **Try only wrapping the lower portion of the body with the arms free.**
- **Provide full body deep pressure touch and massage as an alternative in providing the much needed sensory nutrition achieved through swaddling.**
- **Try using a cuddle/lycra type swing.**
- **With direction supervision, use a memory foam beanbag or squish box for the full flexion and full body deep pressure touch.**

Difficulty Learning to Sit Independently

Sensory Explanation: There can be a few different sensory explanations for this, including a combination of these possibilities. In order to sit independently, the vestibular and proprioceptive systems must be working efficiently and processing information correctly. Sitting involves normalized muscle tone, as well as activation and firing of the proper trunk and pelvic muscles...all which involve proprioceptive feedback. Balance and fine tuning of the vestibular system are also needed for independent sitting.

Ideas to Help!

- A PT or OT evaluation may be indicated if muscle tone imbalance or other unexplained neuromuscular concerns are suspected.
- Use a Boppy® pillow for assisted sitting on a flat, even, firm surface.
- Provide regular and frequent doses of swinging and movement throughout the day.
- Try a weighted lap pad or weighted belt draped over the hips to give the lower body proprioceptive feedback while practicing sitting.
- Work on development of the trunk and pelvic muscles by using a therapy ball or peanut ball for fun interactive play.
- Limit the time the baby is in car seats or bucket type seats, and increase the amount of floor time. Rolling and tummy time all work on the muscles needed for sitting!

Very Slow to Achieve Gross Motor Milestones such as Rolling, Crawling, or Walking

Sensory Explanation: All gross motor milestones require the brain and body to be communicating efficiently and effectively like a well-oiled machine. Even if one sensory system is not processing correctly or at the same pace as the others, it can cause for a delay in achievement of gross motor milestones. There are many other explanations for a delay in gross motor skills, but sensory processing difficulty can often be a significant factor. The vestibular and proprioceptive systems play the biggest role in this.

Ideas to Help!

- A PT or OT evaluation is recommended to assess a possible muscle tone imbalance or other unexplained neuromuscular concerns which may be the root of the delay.
- Focus on the power sensations and the root of development by providing daily and frequent doses of vestibular, proprioceptive, and tactile based play.
- Encourage lots and lots of swinging and movement based play.
- Allow for tons of floor time and tummy time!
- It's quality vs. quantity. Don't rush crawling if rolling and sitting skills have not been refined and developed properly. The brain and nervous system have a reason for the developmental sequence of skills.

Frequent Sneezing

Sensory Explanation: Frequent sneezing can be a systemic reaction to sensory overload or sensory dysregulation. It is important to take this in to consideration if and when allergies and illness have been ruled out.

Ideas to Help!

- When unexplained sneezing occurs, assess the sensory environment closely for triggers. Odd or strong smells would be the first area to assess. Are there strong perfumes or air fresheners? Strong smells from the kitchen?
- If strong smells are ruled out, is the environment too loud or bright? Is there too much social interaction or handling of the baby?
- If sensory overload or dysregulation is suspected, provide a calm and quiet space providing full body deep pressure touch with the little one in full body flexion, such as swaddling or using a soft sling baby carrier.
- If your baby does best being alone during times of sensory overload, create a safe and quiet sensory retreat.
- A cuddle/lycra type swing can be a great way to recover from sensory overload…providing gentle, rhythmical swinging or no swinging at all, just suspended in the swing.

Excessive Sleeping (Shutdown)

Sensory Explanation: Sometimes the only way the nervous system can cope with sensory overload and sensory dysregulation is to sleep and shut out all of the sensory input. During sleep, the brain has time to sort out all of the incoming sensory messages, those which were coming in too fast for the little one's brain to process. This tends to happen more for babies who over-register sensory information or those who struggle with sensory modulation.

Ideas to Help!

- Use this as your sensory cue and signal to decrease the overall amount of sensory input throughout the day, yet providing the types of sensory input that are calming, organizing, and regulating for the nervous system.
- Provide regular and frequent doses of full body deep pressure touch.
- Emphasize full body flexion positioning through swaddling or a soft baby carrier.
- Watch for the signs and sensory triggers that tend to bring on the sensory overload and shutdown and adjust accordingly.
- Limit the running around from place to place. Plan errands when the baby is with another family member or caregiver if possible.
- Try to slow the day down, and be sure to leave plenty of time to just be at home or outdoors at home.

Unusually Short Periods of Sleep

Sensory Explanation: The sleep/wake cycle is directly linked to self-regulation, which is directly linked to sensory processing. If the brain and nervous system are not processing the sensory messages coming in correctly, it is not giving the brain the sensory nutrition it needs to self-regulate, and in turn stay asleep. Another sensory explanation can be sensory over-registration of one or more sensory systems…such as vestibular input (movement). If the baby is extra sensitive to movement, when they shift in position in their sleep it may wake them up. The same applies to tactile input, such as a change in position or changes the amount/type of tactile input. Proprioceptive input and deep pressure touch play the greatest roles in a healthy sleep/wake cycle and sometimes even the shifting of the position of the blanket or the child rolling from leaning on the edge of the crib, to not leaning on it, can change the amount of beneficial proprioceptive input and/or deep pressure touch to cause the little one to wake up.

Ideas to Help!

- **Try using a suspended bassinet or baby hammock, as the gentle vestibular input it provides can be a very powerful tool for assisting with self-regulation.**
- **Immediately prior to naps or nighttime, swing the infant in a soft blanket with slow gentle movements or gentle swinging in a different swing.**
- **A vibrating crib mattress can be very helpful for some babies.**
- **Use a white noise machine or soft instrumental music to help soothe and regulate.**
- **Try a Slumber Bear or other stuffed animal that has a soothing heartbeat feature.**
- **Use tight fitting pajamas for the deep pressure touch.**
- **Use an essential oil diffuser in the room with lavender or other calming oils.**

Dislikes Diaper Changes

Sensory Explanation: Sometimes there is a real simple explanation for this. Little ones, especially the busy and active explorers, simply do not want to be held down or requested to stop doing what they should be doing . . . exploring their world. But sometimes there is much more to it from a sensory standpoint. If there is sensitivity to movement and/or tactile input or even smell or visual input, a diaper change can be a very uncomfortable and even painful experience. It may be that the quick change in position to lying flat on the back is not tolerated well by the vestibular system. It may be the use of the wipes on the skin, feeling like sandpaper on an underdeveloped or over-sensitive tactile system. It may be the increase in strong odor exposed once the diaper is removed. One last thing to consider is the change in lighting, which may simply be too bright with the change in position.

Ideas to Help!

- Carefully assess the situation and try to determine which of the sensory components listed above might be the trigger for disliking diaper changes.
- For the little mover and shaker: immediately prior to the diaper change provide about 5 minutes of vestibular input, such as bouncing, hanging upside down, etc. Also, during the diaper change provide deep pressure touch to the arms and legs or use a vibrating toy or pillow to provide sensory input and a nice distraction. Speaking of distractions…even making silly faces or singing songs may be enough to get you through the diaper change.
- If movement is not tolerated well, try using a slight incline or at least a pillow so the head does not have to be completely flat. Also, transition to the laying on back position very slowly while holding the body very firm.
- If the wipes seem to be the trigger…maybe they need a change in temperature to be tolerated. Or perhaps it is the smell. Try unscented.
- If the strong odor seems to be a trigger, offer a soft toy for the baby to play with that has a couple of drops of a pleasant essential oil.
- If the baby is sensitive to light, turn off overhead lighting and instead use a soft lamp or natural light.

Dislikes Laying on Back

Sensory Explanation: The vestibular system is a very complex and sensitive system. The baby may not be able to tolerate the head and body in this position, especially if a quick change in position is involved. Another sensory factor may be visual input…the type and intensity of visual input changes when lying on the back.

Ideas to Help!

- When needing to lay the little one on her back, do it very slowly while holding the body firmly and cradling the head in your hand, even if the baby can support the head independently. Doing this will help the nervous system adjust to the change in body position.
- Use a pillow or an inclined surface rather than flat on the back.
- Tolerating movement is VERY critical to overall development, so an assessment by an OT trained in sensory integration is strongly recommended.
- In the meantime offer different types of movement that are tolerated well.
- Offer swinging in a blanket or cuddle/lycra type swing. When deep pressure touch and proprioception are incorporated into movement, the vestibular system tends to tolerate and accept it better.

Constant Need for Thumb Sucking/Pacifier

Sensory Explanation: The oral sensory system and the suck/swallow/breathe pattern are the two most common and beneficial ways for an infant to self-regulate and self-soothe…it begins in utero. It is essential and critical for overall infant development. Some children continue with this primitive self-regulating and soothing strategy way past the infant stages. This may be the case due to under-registration of the oral sensory system, therefore the brain and nervous system need more and more of it to meet the brain's requirements. Or other sensory systems, such as the proprioceptive and vestibular systems, may not be processing correctly, and the oral sensory system is over-compensating to help with self-regulation.

Ideas to Help!

- **Respect this as a sensory need and allow the use of a pacifier as needed.**
- **Try substituting with an oral sensory tool.**
- **If the little one is old enough, try bubble mountain.**
- **Encourage basic musical instruments that require blowing.**
- **Encourage resistive sucking, such as yogurt or pudding through a straw.**
- **Encourage the use of a straw or curly/twisty straw.**
- **If the little one is able, use a child size Camelbak® water bottle.**
- **Be sure to enrich the day with plenty of play opportunities involving the vestibular and proprioceptive systems.**

Needs VERY Big Movements to Soothe and Calm (rocking, swinging, bouncing)

Sensory Explanation: If the vestibular system is under-registering information, the brain may need very intense and powerful forms of movement to actually feel it. The brain and nervous system rely on vestibular input as one of the primary sources to assist in self-regulation and neurobehavioral organization for infants.

Ideas to Help!

- Provide ongoing and frequent doses of movement based play and activities throughout the day . . . the more the better.
- Limit the time that the little one is in a car seat, other baby seat, or carrier. Instead, increase the amount of floor time and active play.
- Go on daily walks in the stroller or in a wagon. Make it bumpy and swerve if your baby responds well to this!
- Invert the head frequently. Hold the baby upside down or tip back over your knees while seated. Head inversion provides very powerful vestibular input.
- An exercise/therapy ball would be a great way to play and interact for powerful movement.
- Bounce, bounce, and bounce some more! Vertical vestibular is very organizing and regulating for the brain.
- Swinging the baby in different body positions and different planes of movement will help the brain learn to register vestibular input. Try swinging in prone, side lying, sitting, and supine. Using a cuddle type swing or swinging in a blanket is a good tool for this.

Turns Body and Head Away from Caregiver when Bottle Feeding

Sensory Explanation: This can be due to a variety of factors. One being that eye contact is not comfortable for the little one. Secondly, it may be related to tactile input from the face touching or brushing against the caregiver's clothing or skin and turning away from the situation decreases the input. Same goes for olfactory input (smell). The infant may not tolerate the different smells associated with the caregiver such as perfume, lotion, deodorant, fabric scents, etc. Or possibly the turning of the head in a certain direction is uncomfortable to the vestibular system. One last explanation could be the entire experience is too overwhelming for the infant and offers too many forms of sensory input, so the social interaction component is simply too much to handle while the baby is focused on eating.

Ideas to Help!

- **Try switching to the other side while holding the baby to bottle feed, as it may be the position of the head that is uncomfortable.**
- **Try using a supportive pillow like a Boppy®.**
- **Drape a familiar and favorite blanket that the baby loves over your shoulder to provide a soothing texture. This will also decrease the possible unfamiliar or strong smells from the caregiver, which will be replaced with the scent of the blanket.**
- **If the baby seems to shift eye contact, offer only occasional and fleeting eye contact. Instead, sing soft and soothing songs while feeding or just be present, but silent, in the moment.**
- **Gently rock while feeding in a nice quiet and dimly lit room.**

Needs Cheeks Stuffed Very Full to Chew and Swallow

Sensory Explanation: This can be due to under-registration of tactile and proprioceptive input of the oral structures and jaw joints. When the cheeks are stuffed full, it provides increased proprioceptive input, tactile input and deep pressure touch, which provides the brain the cues and signals it needs to activate the muscles needed to chew and swallow.

Ideas to Help!

- Encourage regular and frequent use of a Z-Vibe® or other vibrating oral sensory tool, especially prior to mealtime.
- Offer various oral sensory tools with different textures.
- Provide regular, daily if possible, full body messy play opportunities. This will help the overall tactile system process information more efficiently.
- If the little one is able to use a straw, provide resistive sucking activities such as pudding or yogurt through a straw.
- Encourage resistive blowing activities such as a baby harmonica or horn.
- Direct and constant supervision for the little one during eating is strongly recommended, as the risk of choking is much greater.
- Always cut food into small pieces, and monitor or ration throughout the meal.
- Providing firm pressure to the cheeks, jaw line, and throat prior to the meal can be helpful in giving the mouth structure. This can also be helpful to facilitate the actual swallow.

Extreme Difficulty with Falling Asleep

Sensory Explanation: The sleep/wake cycle relies on so many sensory components, all which play a role in self-regulation and neurobehavioral organization. If one or more sensory systems are not processing information correctly and efficiently, the brain may not be getting the proper sensory nutrition needed to self-regulate…and in turn support the sleep/wake cycle. Proper sleep patterns also depend on healthy nutrition and sensory enrichment throughout the day.

Ideas to Help!

- Try using a suspended bassinet or baby hammock, as the gentle vestibular input it provides can be a very powerful tool for assisting with self-regulation.
- Immediately prior to naps or nighttime, swing the infant in a soft blanket with slow gentle movements or gentle swinging in a different swing.
- A vibrating crib mattress can be very helpful for some babies.
- Use a white noise machine or soft instrumental music to help soothe and regulate.
- Try a Slumber Bear or other stuffed animal that has a soothing heartbeat feature.
- Use tight fitting pajamas for the deep pressure touch.
- Use an essential oil diffuser in the room with lavender or other calming oils.
- Limit the amount of screen time (none is best) and instead replace with active floor time and exploratory play.
- Outside time is essential everyday as well as safe amounts of sunlight.
- Provide whole, organic foods and proper hydration with filtered pure water.

Unable to Self-Soothe

Sensory Explanation: Babies are able to self-soothe within the womb, in an environment which provides the perfect, safe, just-right amount of sensory input. This also includes an increasing amount of proprioception as the fetus is tucked in full body flexion as it grows and the living space gets smaller. This "squish" is key in self-soothing. When the baby is born it is thrown in to a world of bright lights, loud sounds, different textures, constant change of position, etc. What a drastic change! Infants need our assistance to self-soothe as their little nervous system continues to develop in a not so friendly sensory world.

Ideas to Help!

- Provide frequent and daily opportunities for swaddling.
- Regularly use a soft sling baby carrier.
- Use a baby hammock or cuddle/lycra-type swing.
- Provide full body deep pressure touch many times each day.
- Maintain a calm, quiet, dimly and naturally lit home environment.
- Turn off the TV and replace it with soft instrumental music.
- Limit the transitions and time spent taking the baby from place to place in the baby seat/carrier.
- Offer an oral sensory tool for access at all times.
- Provide gentle, rhythmic swinging often throughout the day.

Dislikes Being Touched and/or Held; Calms When Put Down

Sensory Explanation: This can be an indicator that the tactile system is not processing correctly and is over-registering and sensitive to touch. Touch, especially light touch, can be very uncomfortable and even painful for the baby. There can be other sensory factors involved when holding the baby, such as the movement you are providing or the body position. Light, sound, and smell can also be factors which make being helped uncomfortable for the little one.

Ideas to Help!

- Become very in tune to the type of touch you provide, refrain from light touch, and replace with deep pressure touch and firm pressure.
- Use firm even hugs and holding/cuddling, with or without movement, whichever the baby best responds to.
- Provide daily doses of full body deep pressure touch and baby massage if the little one tolerates and enjoys it.
- Increase the amount of swaddling and use of a soft sling baby carrier.
- Try snug fitting long-sleeved and long-legged clothing to help dampen the tactile receptors.
- Offer regular opportunities for tactile based play, beginning with dry textures and working towards messy textures…never force this type of activity. Let the baby explore independently.

Prefers Being in the Dark When Awake

Sensory Explanation: This is a very likely indicator that the baby is having a difficult time with visual processing and tolerance of light. The visual system is over-registering incoming visual messages which can include light, color, objects, etc. In the dark, not only is light decreased to a comfortable level, the amount of visible visual input is also decreased.

Ideas to Help!

- **Offer and honor this opportunity when possible.**
- **Begin to naturally introduce more light and visual input via soft lamp lighting and natural light.**
- **Turn off overhead lighting and definitely refrain from using fluorescent lights.**
- **When outdoors or in the community be proactive by having your baby wear a floppy type hat or fisherman's hat to decrease the visual input.**
- **Baby sunglasses are also a good idea.**
- **Declutter and organize the home and rooms where the baby spends the most time.**
- **Neutral and pastel colors for the walls are best.**

Head Being Tipped Backwards Is Not Tolerated Well

Sensory Explanation: This can be related to vestibular defensiveness/over-registration and difficulty processing movement. The brain detects and processes movement via the semicircular canals in the ears, so a change in head position is just like moving the baby's entire body. Head inversion, which is the position achieved when the head is tipped backwards, is a very powerful sensation and must be respected as such for infants. Another factor in this not being tolerated is the other forms of sensory input involved when the head is tipped back (such as water on the face or head for a bath).

Ideas to Help!

- Tolerating movement is critical for all aspects of development, so an assessment by an OT specializing in sensory integration is strongly recommended.
- Provide daily opportunities for swinging in various planes of movement and with the body in different positions, such as reclined back or lying on the stomach . . . swinging side to side, back and forth, and diagonals. Do this in very small doses that are tolerated by the child. Never force it. Using a blanket to swing the baby in is a great tool for this.
- Use a therapy ball or peanut ball and lay the baby on his back, slowly working towards a greater inverted angle. Use firm pressure to the entire body to help provide security and a dose of full body deep pressure touch and proprioception to help with this new sensory experience.
- With the little one is sitting on your lap facing you, hold the forearms and slowly tip backwards, singing songs and making it playful. Watch closely for signs of resistance and stop at that point.
- Provide full body deep pressure touch in regular doses, including swaddling throughout the day.
- A cuddle/lycra swing is a great tool to help the vestibular system slowly learn to process and accept movement.

Will Only Breastfeed in the Dark

Sensory Explanation: The most likely sensory explanation for this is the infant is not tolerating visual input well, and therefore needs a very low visual stimuli environment to focus and self-regulate while nursing. This can also simply be a sensory preference for the baby who finds it more soothing and comforting nursing in the dark.

Ideas to Help!

- Respect this as a true sensory need, and honor this whenever possible.
- Even in the privacy of your home, try using a breastfeeding/nursing cover-up, one dark in color to block out all light.
- Try using a nursing/breastfeeding hat. These hats are big, floppy, beach-type hats made specifically for the baby. They provide privacy for nursing, but also will block out all light, creating a dark place for the little one.
- Along with low lighting, try other soothing and calming sensory techniques such as deep pressure touch, gentle rocking, instrumental music, or a weighted lap pad while nursing.
- Decrease the overall amount of sensory input during nursing to help the infant self-regulate.

Excessive Bouncing, Including Bouncing on Bottom Across the Floor

Sensory Explanation: Bouncing provides vertical vestibular input, one of the most tolerated planes of vestibular input. Bouncing also provides a dose of joint compression to the neck/spine and to the lower body joints if the little one is bouncing while assisted in a standing position (such as a Johnny Jump Up® or Rody). Both of these forms of sensory input are very organizing and regulating for the nervous system. Another explanation may be that the baby is under-registering sensory input in these areas, and constant and excessive bouncing helps feed the brain the sensory nutrition it is craving.

Ideas to Help!

- Bounce, bounce, and bounce some more!
- Provide various sensory tools and toys that encourage bouncing and jumping such as Rody or a Johnny Jump Up®.
- Encourage vestibular input in other planes of movement, such as rocking, swaying side to side, and standard swinging.
- Gently invert the little one's head if tolerated well.
- Use a therapy ball or peanut ball for bouncing and interactive vestibular play.
- Limit time in stationary toys and carriers, and replace with floor time and active exploratory play.
- Take daily walks outdoors in a stroller or wagon . . . the bumpier the ride the better!

Dislikes Car Seats, Particularly Backward Facing

Sensory Explanation: Riding in the car provides constantly changing vestibular input, from the changing speeds of the moving vehicle to the turns and curves, all which may or may not be tolerated by the very young and developing nervous system of an infant. And backward facing offers an entirely different sensory experience, and is even more likely to not be tolerated well by a vestibular system which is already showing difficulty in processing. The other factor possibly playing a role is the straps of the car seat that may be touching the face and neck, both which can be very sensitive for babies.

Ideas to Help!

- Place blackout shields on the windows. This can help decrease the visual input which can trigger a negative vestibular response.
- Use a vibrating pillow or toy if this is calming to the infant during car rides.
- If using an infant car seat, drape it with a lightweight blanket or cover to decrease the visual input.
- Try a head snuggler for the car seat to provide a gentle head compression and deep pressure touch by stabilizing the head during transport.
- Provide a pacifier or other oral sensory tool to help calm and soothe the nervous system.
- If movement is not tolerated well overall, an evaluation by a sensory integration OT is strongly recommended.

Dislikes Sleep Sacks and/or Pajamas with Feet

Sensory Explanation: Some little ones simply do not like to be confined, so they prefer to be all spread out and wiggling as they wish. This is just a sensory preference. There may also be a sensory explanation for this, such as tactile defensiveness/over-registration of tactile input. The feeling and texture of the sleep sack or footed pajamas may be uncomfortable on the skin or even painful.

Ideas to Help!

- **Try snug fitting pajamas instead of the sleep sack or pajamas with feet. The snug fit of the clothing provides deep pressure touch to the body, which can be regulating for the nervous system and also dampen the tactile receptors of the skin if they are over-registering.**
- **Provide regular daily doses of deep pressure touch to the arms, legs, hands, and feet.**
- **Provide daily opportunities for full body tactile play, working from dry mediums to messy...this will help the tactile system learn to process information more efficiently.**

Constant Movement of Arms and Legs

Sensory Explanation: This is to be expected with a very young baby when the brain and body is learning to coordinate and independently use the muscles of the arms and legs. A baby who does this after the initial phase of development may be seeking out proprioceptive input to the arms and legs. It may feel good to the brain and body and can be a way to soothe, calm, and self-regulate.

Ideas to Help!

- If this type of movement persists and appears involuntary in nature past the first few months of development, an evaluation by a pediatric OT or PT is strongly recommended to rule out any neurological or neuromuscular concerns unrelated to sensory integration.
- Provide full body deep pressure touch on a daily and frequent basis along with plenty of swaddling.
- Swinging in a blanket or cuddle/lycra swing provides proprioception and deep pressure and can be very regulating for the little one.
- Provide toys that encourage banging.
- Limit the time spent in stationary carriers or toys, and instead encourage active floor time play.
- For older babies, encourage bouncing and jumping type play as well as weight bearing through the arms and legs such as using a resistance tunnel, Rody, or use of a therapy/exercise ball.

Tensing Up or Shaking of the Hands

Sensory Explanation: This can be a sign of sensory overload or sensory overstimulation, although for an infant it could simply be a sign of excitement and joy. When the brain and body is still learning how to coordinate purposeful movements of the arms and hands, it may present as tensing up and shaking. It is often a way to "release" some of the intense excitement and emotion that may be developing in any given moment or situation. If this persists or seems involuntary in nature, it is important to rule out a neurological or neuromuscular condition unrelated to sensory processing.

Ideas to Help!

- Decrease the overall amount of sensory input if the little one seems dysregulated or distressed along with the shivering or shaking of the hands.
- Offer a calm and quiet space to see if this resolves the symptoms.
- Provide deep pressure touch to the arms and hands.
- For babies old enough to grasp/squeeze/ manipulate objects…offer heavy work activities such as push and pull movement-based play or squeeze-type fidget toys to provide proprioception to the hands and arms.
- If this persists or seems involuntary in nature, an evaluation by an OT or PT is recommended.

Dislikes Riding in the Car at Night

Sensory Explanation: If this sensory signal only presents itself at night, it may be due to the change in visual input…the darkness along with flickering and bright lights and movement of the car may simply be too much for the visual system at a young age. The baby may also be having difficulty processing vestibular input (movement) overall. If you feel this is the case, an evaluation by a sensory trained OT is recommended.

Ideas to Help!

- Block out the bright lights and flickering by using window shades or covering the car seat.
- Try using a hat or hood to block out some of the light.
- Try infant sunglasses, even when it is dark out.
- Offer other calming tools when in the car such as a vibrating toy or pillow, oral sensory tool, musical toy, or favorite comfort item.
- Cover the car seat with a light weight blanket to decrease the visual stimuli.

Dislikes Outfit Changes and Certain Clothing

Sensory Explanation: This can be explained by more than one sensory trigger. The tactile system is possibly over-registering and feels the texture of every square inch of the fabric and it may be painful or uncomfortable. (Certain textures likely more than others). The other factor may be related to vestibular sensitivity and the quick and frequent changes in body position during a clothing change.

Ideas to Help!

- Rule out the vestibular component by limiting movement of the head and body as much as possible during the clothing change. Also, try supported sitting to complete the clothing change rather than lying down. See if this improves the situation.
- Assess the textures of clothing that the little one seems to react to the most and replace with the textures easily tolerated. This is not something that the baby will just "get used to".
- Remove tags on clothing or use Undercover Tape™ to cover the itchy tags and seams that may be bothersome.
- Use underclothing that is snug fitting to provide calming input to the tactile system and dampen the tactile receptors.

Shuts Down in Social Situations Outside of the Home

Sensory Explanation: Social situations, especially in the community and in unfamiliar environments outside the comfort of home, offer an extreme amount of unpredictable, unexpected, and unfamiliar multi-sensory input. (Many sounds, unexpected hugs, kisses, passing the infant around to hold and handle, etc.) Shutting down is a coping strategy for the nervous system when the incoming sensory input is simply too much to handle and process.

Ideas to Help!

- Keep this in mind anytime you are outside of the home, and monitor and limit the amount of multi-sensory input.
- One of the most overwhelming forms of input is the social interaction component. Simply explain to others that the baby is very sensitive to sensory input, and ask that they honor and limit the direct social interaction.
- When in the community and social situations, use a soft sling baby carrier to provide calming and regulating input for the little one to cope with the multi-sensory input.
- A stroller or carrier covered up can be helpful.
- Provide additional calming sensory tools such as a comfort item, vibrating toy, or oral sensory tool.
- Try Baby Banz noise cancelling headphones or a snug hat that covers the ears to decrease auditory input.
- Try baby sunglasses or a hat to decrease visual input.

Not Mouthing Objects

Sensory Explanation: Oral sensory development and mouthing objects is a very critical component for infant development. If a baby does not mouth objects it may be due to an over-responsive oral sensory system, involving both tactile input and possibly gustatory and olfactory senses. The mouth is full of tactile receptors. If they are over-registering information, it may be uncomfortable or painful to the nervous system when new textures and objects are placed in or near the mouth. It may also be a combination of this along with not tolerating new taste and smell, or it can be just one of these 3 components.

Ideas to Help!

- Since this is a critical stage of development, an evaluation by a sensory integration OT is strongly recommended if this persists. The sooner the better.
- Offer various oral sensory tools of different textures.
- Try oral sensory tools that provide inviting scents.
- Provide deep pressure touch to the facial structures and around the mouth as tolerated on a daily and regular basis.
- Offer a Z-Vibe®, children's vibrating toothbrush, or other vibrating oral sensory tool. Sometimes the baby will tolerate vibration better than other forms of sensory input.
- Provide daily opportunities for messy play and food related play. Make it fun and interactive!
- Never force any of the above ideas and activities. Watch closely for the baby's reaction and sensory cues to determine if it is being accepted by the nervous system as safe and comfortable.

Limp/Floppy Body

Sensory Explanation: If this presents after the first month of life, it may be due to under-registration of proprioceptive feedback from the muscles and joints, as well as a sluggish vestibular system which has difficulty detecting changes in posture or position in space. This is a very critical indicator for early intervention. This can also be related to other neurological or neuromuscular conditions, so be sure that these have been ruled out.

Ideas to Help!

- An evaluation by an OT and a PT is strongly recommended, the sooner the better.
- Offer frequent doses of vestibular input throughout the day, offering movement in all directions and planes...such as bouncing, side to side, back and forth, and diagonal planes. Only swing in the directions tolerated well by the baby.
- Emphasize floor time, especially tummy time.
- Limit time spent in carriers and bucket type seats, and instead replace with floor time.
- Offer frequent doses throughout the day of full body deep pressure touch and baby massage.
- Encourage full body flexion via swaddling or in a soft sling carrier. This will also provide proprioceptive feedback to the body.

Lacks Awareness of Body in Space and Body Position

Sensory Explanation: This is very typical and common for babies and toddlers as they are just learning to put it all together with a constantly changing and growing body. It is important to see steady progress in this area. If not, the little one may be struggling with proprioceptive awareness and feedback. It may also be due to poor vestibular registration.

Ideas to Help!

- Provide daily doses of full body deep pressure touch and baby massage.
- Provide frequent swaddling and use of a soft sling carrier with the baby in full body flexion.
- Offer daily swinging in different planes of movement.
- A cuddle/lycra swing is a great way to provide both vestibular and proprioceptive input.
- Provide daily stroller or wagon rides over bumpy surfaces.
- Limit time in stationary toys, and increase the amount of floor time and exploratory play.

Arches Back Often

Sensory Explanation: Arching the back provides proprioceptive input to the spine and trunk as well as vestibular input from the change in body position. Arching can also indicate pain or discomfort somewhere within the gut, which needs to be addressed and ruled out. Sometimes arching is more of an involuntary response by the neuromuscular system from high muscle tone or abnormal muscle tone. This needs to be assessed by an OT or PT as well, to rule out a condition unrelated to sensory processing.

Ideas to Help!

- Rule out digestive issues or other abdominal triggers.
- An evaluation by an OT or PT is recommended if this persists and other developmental delays are present.
- See if providing deep pressure touch or swaddling decreases the arching.
- Swing the baby in a blanket or baby hammock.
- Try vertical vestibular input using a therapy ball or peanut ball, or simply try gentle bouncing on your lap.
- Invert the baby's head slightly while supporting the body and neck, then return to upright position very slowly.

Loud or Unexpected Sounds Are Startling or Cause Fear

Sensory Explanation: This is to be expected for very young infants, causing the startle (Moro) reflex. The startle reflex should integrate and disappear by 3-4 months of age. If startling, yet not observed as the true Moro reflex continues, this can be caused by an auditory system that over-registers input as well as possible difficulty with self-regulation. If the nervous system is having a tough time regulating and processing incoming sensory information, unexpected and loud sounds can be overwhelming. A baby who over-registers auditory input may be unable to filter out irrelevant sounds, frequencies, tones, and pitch.

Ideas to Help!

- If the startle (Moro) reflex persists beyond 4 months of age, an evaluation by an OT or PT is strongly recommended.
- Try noise cancelling headphones, such as Baby Banz, to help decrease the auditory input.
- When outside of the home particularly, be proactive and either use the noise cancelling headphones or decrease the auditory input by having the baby wear a snug hat that pulls down over the ears.
- Provide daily and frequent movement activities, as vestibular input helps with auditory processing.

Frequently Rubs Ears and Head

Sensory Explanation: This may be an indicator of a headache, ear infection, or other illness, so be sure that these medical reasons are ruled out. From a sensory standpoint, doing this provides proprioception and deep pressure touch, as well as unique auditory input when done to the ears. This can be a strategy for self-regulating. Another explanation is that it is an indicator of sensory overload from sound, or may also be due to generalized sensory overload. It is also very common for infants to rub their ears and head when tired and trying to transition to sleep.

Ideas to Help!

- Provide regular doses of deep pressure touch to the head, ears, and cheeks.
- Provide head compressions via gentle pressure to the top of the head.
- If sensory overload and sensitivity seems to be the trigger, try noise cancelling headphones with sunglasses or a floppy hat.
- If out in the community and the baby is in a stroller or car seat, use a cover to help decrease sensory input.
- Invert the head slightly with support of the neck and head if tolerated well.
- Try a vibrating pillow or toy.
- Provide an oral sensory tool, including one that vibrates.
- Increase the amount of swinging and movement throughout the day.
- Try using a hat that offers compression and slight pressure to the head, as well as one that pulls down over the ears.
- If it seems like this is a signal of being tired, offer a calm, dark, quiet, cozy space for a nap.
- Swaddling and/or use of a soft sling carrier can also be very helpful.

Head Banging (against walls, crib, etc)

Sensory Explanation: Although unsafe and concerning, head banging tends to be an effective way for a baby to help self-regulate. It does provide a powerful dose of proprioceptive to the neck joints as well as vestibular input. It also provides a version of a head compression (which is also proprioception). When a little one is doing this it is likely to help calm, soothe, fall asleep, or even to maintain an alert state. It is also very important to rule out any medical or other neurological concerns. An evaluation by your primary health care provider, along with an OT or PT evaluation is recommended.

Ideas to Help!

- A soft conforming protective helmet is strongly recommended to be worn at all times if the baby does this on a regular basis. This will also provide deep pressure touch to the head, which can decrease the urge to bang the head.
- Provide regular and frequent gentle head compressions.
- Offer a vibrating toy or pillow.
- Invert the baby's head slightly while supporting the head, neck, and shoulders. Come back to upright slowly.
- Use a therapy or exercise ball to provide vestibular input in the planes of movement that the baby likes best.
- Provide frequent doses of swinging and other forms of movement throughout the day.
- Limit time in stationary carriers and toys, and increase the amount of floor time and active play.

Loves to Get Messy and Engage in Full Body Messy Play

Sensory Explanation: Full body messy play is an extremely therapeutic, powerful sensory experience and critical for development! It is important for development of the tactile system, as well as to support development of body in space, tactile discrimination, and body awareness. When a baby seeks out this activity in an intense fashion, it can indicate that the tactile system is under-registering tactile input. The little one, therefore, craves it and needs it in very intense doses to actually feel it and register the tactile input. On the other hand, thoroughly enjoying and craving full body messy play is also a very natural stage in development.

Ideas to Help!

- The messier the better!
- Encourage daily opportunities for full body messy play. Use safe, preferably organic (at least all natural) mediums for this, such as yogurt or pudding.
- Use the bathtub without water in it as the messy play zone. Creating a parent friendly/easy clean-up messy play area will increase the likelihood for daily opportunities of messy play.
- Encourage other full body types of tactile based play, such as sand or dry lentils. Direct supervision is recommended to be sure the child is not putting these in the mouth.
- If the weather is conducive, messy play outdoors is a great way to incorporate interacting with and exploring nature. Make some mud pudding. ☺

Always Holds a Special Object or Blanket

Sensory Explanation: This is very common for babies, and can be soothing and calming for them. It provides a sense of control within the environment, whereas the rest of the world can be a very unpredictable, scary, and uncomfortable place. This can also provide a comforting form of tactile and/or olfactory input.

Ideas to Help!

- Respect it as a sensory need that assists with self-regulation.
- Try various fidget toys as alternatives.
- Add a couple drops of a calming essential oil to the fabric to increase the self-regulatory benefit.
- If the little one has a particular object or blanket that is the favorite, I strongly advise that you go and buy at least 2-3 more of the item if available. You will thank me in the long run on this one. ☺

Best with Breastfeeding or a Bottle When Drowsy or Asleep

Sensory Explanation: A baby may do this if they struggle with self-regulation and neurobehavioral organization. The suck/swallow/breathe sequence is very regulating and soothing for the nervous system. Another possible explanation may be that the baby is distracted by the increased amount of sensory input when awake, making it difficult to focus on the task at hand which is eating.

Ideas to Help!

- Breast or bottle feed in a quiet space with minimal natural lighting.
- Try white noise or soft instrumental music.
- Try a rocking chair.
- Use a Boppy® pillow and a breastfeeding cover to further decrease the sensory input and to provide full body deep pressure touch to the body while feeding.
- Try a weighted lap pad, under direction of a sensory integration OT.
- Provide calming and rhythmical swinging in a baby hammock or lycra/cuddle type swing prior to the feeding.

Stiffens Body or Arches during Breast or Bottle Feedings

Sensory Explanation: Arching and stiffening of the body are quite often sensory signals of discomfort in some way. It may be related to the vestibular system and position of the body and head or a GI discomfort, such as reflux or gas. It could also be a sign that the baby is trying to self-regulate in order to organize the suck/swallow/breathe pattern and is moving the body to help with neurobehavioral organization.

Ideas to Help!

- If the arching and stiffening of the body occurs at other times as well and seems involuntary in nature, an evaluation by an OT or PT is recommended to rule out other neurological or neuromuscular concerns unrelated to sensory triggers.
- Try a Boppy® pillow.
- Try elevating the position of the head.
- Does the little one feed better facing one direction vs. the other? I know this can only be accommodated with bottle feeds.
- Try deep pressure touch to the arms, hands, feet, and legs during the feeding.
- Try a vibrating pillow.
- Minimize the overall sensory input…feed in a calm, quiet, and dimly lit space.
- Try gentle rocking during feeding.

Latches and Unlatches during Breast Feeding or Bottle Feeding

Sensory Explanation: The suck/swallow/breathe pattern is much more complex than one might think. If the infant is struggling with neurobehavioral organization (self-regulation), this skill can be extremely difficult. So when the baby is latching on and off, he may be needing a "breather" to coordinate the swallowing and breathing part of the sequence. Another sensory explanation can be that the tactile and proprioceptive receptors in and surrounding the mouth are under-registering and can't "feel" what to do and latch on properly. The mouth and lips may not be getting the correct amount of feedback.

Ideas to Help!

- Prior to feeding, provide deep pressure touch to the cheeks, jawline, and perioral muscle around the mouth.
- Also prior to feeding use a Z-Vibe® or other oral sensory tool that provides vibration, if the infant tolerates this well.
- Before feeding provide 15 minutes of vestibular input…swinging, bouncing, swaying, etc.
- Be sure the body and neck are supported well and in slight neck/head flexion.
- Feed in a calm and quiet space.

Searches Frantically When Trying to Latch for Breastfeeding

Sensory Explanation: The tactile and proprioceptive receptors surrounding the mouth may be under-registering and can't "feel" what to do and latch on properly. The cheeks, mouth, and lips may not be getting the correct amount of feedback to tell the brain it is time to latch on. Another explanation may be that the little one is having a difficult time with self-regulation and neurobehavioral organization, and the commencement of feeding time is simply too exciting and overwhelming to coordinate and organize the act of latching on to nurse.

Ideas to Help!

- **Prior to feeding, provide deep pressure touch to the cheeks, jawline, and perioral muscle around the mouth.**
- **Also prior to feeding use a Z-Vibe® or other oral sensory tool that provides vibration, if the infant tolerates this well.**
- **Before feeding provide 15 minutes of vestibular input…swinging, bouncing, swaying, etc.**
- **Be sure the body and neck are supported well and in slight neck/head flexion.**
- **Feed in a calm and quiet space.**
- **Play soft, instrumental music during feeding time.**
- **While nursing, try swaddling and full body deep pressure touch to help support self-regulation.**

Needs Constant Swaddling to Stay Calm

Sensory Explanation: Swaddling is quite possibly the most soothing, calming, and regulating sensory tool you can provide for an infant to support self-regulation and neurobehavioral organization. It provides full body proprioception and deep pressure touch along with the body being in full flexion. These are all very regulating for the brain and nervous system. This is a sensory signal to you that the little one needs quite a bit of support to assist in self-regulation. This is also very common for premature babies since they were not given the full opportunity to be squished into full flexion in the womb.

Ideas to Help!

- Swaddle that little cutie as much as needed, nice and snug with the body, arms, and legs tucked into flexion.
- Use a soft sling carrier, this also provides the same form of sensory input, as well as getting the body into full flexion.
- Use a baby hammock and/or lycra/cuddle type swing.
- Provide daily and frequent doses of full body deep pressure touch.
- Snug, compression type clothing is also a great tool.

Bath Time is Difficult

Sensory Explanation: If your baby is resisting bath time, there is most likely one or more sensory triggers causing the experience to be uncomfortable for the nervous system. There are so many components involved during a bath, so be sure to assess each aspect as a possible trigger.

Ideas to Help!

- If your baby seems sensitive to sound (bathrooms often have an echo), place numerous bathmats or rugs on the floor to help with this. The bathmats and rugs will also help the tactile system and the unexpected change of texture and temperature for little bare feet.
- For newborns, using the portable bathtub in a calm, quiet, and lowly lit room is best.
- Use a baby visor to avoid the unexpected tactile input from the water droplets to the face.
- Try not to adjust and move the baby around too much during the bath. Especially keep the head in one position.
- Determine if the baby prefers to be slightly reclined or assisted in sitting position.
- Natural and organic soaps and shampoos are strongly encouraged.
- Make sure bath time is fun and not rushed; let it be a time to relax and enjoy the water.
- Play relaxing, instrumental music during bath time to promote self-regulation.
- Offer a pacifier or other oral sensory tool to help soothe the baby.
- Use a very soft washcloth if tactile defensiveness is an issue.
- Check the temperature…it can be a big factor if not just right.

Body Feels Stiff and/or Stiffens Frequently

Sensory Explanation: It is important to consult with an OT or PT to rule out other neuromuscular or neurological reasons for the increased muscle tone. If all checks out ok, then sensory factors can be considered as the explanation. The increased muscle tone can be a reaction to the environment or sensory stimuli or as a technique to increase the amount of proprioception to the body. When muscles contract, it stimulates the proprioception receptors and can support self-regulation. So the little one may be using this as a tool to help self-regulate and soothe.

Ideas to Help!

- Begin with an OT or PT evaluation to rule out concerns unrelated to sensory seeking or a self-regulation strategy.
- Provide frequent doses of full body deep pressure touch and baby massage throughout the day.
- Encourage the body position of full flexion by swaddling or using a soft sling carrier or cuddle/lycra swing.
- Try a vibrating pillow to see if it relaxes the body. It may, however, do the opposite. If so, discontinue.
- Assess the environment closely when you see this sensory signal…is there too much input from light, sound, smells, touch, movement, etc?
- Try compression clothing.
- Try a squish box or large memory foam beanbag with the little one positioned in full flexion. Direct supervision is recommended.

Avoids Crawling on All Fours and/or Prefers Scooting on the Bottom

Sensory Explanation: There can be many factors involved with this preference, some strictly sensory and some sensorimotor. From a sensory standpoint…one must consider the vestibular, visual, and tactile systems. The change in head position may not be tolerated well by the vestibular system. Also the visual system may not tolerate and process this different position in prone. The other component to consider is the tactile input to the palms of the hands and also to the knees and legs. From a sensorimotor standpoint, bilateral coordination, shoulder stability, upper and lower body weighted shifting, normalized muscle tone, motor planning, body awareness, body in space, trunk strength, and overall range of motion and strength are all factors to consider.

Ideas to Help!

- It is ok for the little one to scoot, yet crawling has significant benefits in brain development, so it is important to encourage crawling and the four-point position.
- Begin with working in prone (on tummy) over a therapy ball or peanut ball. Make it fun and interactive. Also encourage plenty of tummy time on the floor.
- Encourage weight bearing on arms.
- Determine if there is intolerance to movement which is limiting the child to try the crawling position or a muscle tone imbalance or lack. If so, an OT or PT evaluation is recommended.
- Offer daily and frequent swinging and bouncing opportunities.
- Encourage commando crawling, as this will help develop the foundational skills for four-point crawling.
- Work on the four-point (crawling) in a stationary position, providing the "just right" amount of tactile support under the belly. The weight bearing through all of the joints provides proprioception and will help develop the muscles needed to crawl.

Avoids Facing in When Held, Prefers Facing Outward

Sensory Explanation: This preference can be due to one or more sensory factors: vestibular, tactile, or olfactory sensitivity. Your little one may not tolerate backwards movement or not being able to see where she is going. She may also be avoiding the light touch from your hair or texture of clothing to the face and neck. The smells of your body, detergent, hairspray, etc. will all be less intense when held facing outward as well.

Ideas to Help!

- It's ok. Hold the baby facing outward if that is the preference.
- For the times when holding towards your body is necessary, try to determine if there is a sensory trigger...such as the texture of your clothing or the perfumes, detergent, lotion used.
- Decrease the amount of sensory triggers from yourself. Pull your hair back, and limit any hairspray, perfume, lotion, etc.
- Determine if there is movement intolerance...if so, an evaluation by a sensory integration OT is recommended.
- The baby may also just prefer the visual input involved while being held forward facing and is enjoying the visual information, which is stimulating to the brain. So allow it when possible.

Does Not Like Kisses

Sensory Explanation: Kisses are often not well tolerated since there is unexpected and variable tactile input, along with the close proximity of the person which may also bring along strong smells and a quick change in visual information. Soft kisses activate the light touch receptors and firm kisses activate deep pressure touch receptors. And then you have the variable of a wet or dry kiss. Infants have a tactile system still maturing and learning to process all of the different forms of tactile input along with the other sensory systems. Sometimes the facial tactile receptors are not maturing at the same rate as the rest of the tactile system and the kiss can truly be painful and uncomfortable.

Ideas to Help!

- Respect this as a true sensory difference, and instead provide affection via hugs, cuddling, singing, rocking, and talking with the little one. Give the tactile system more time to develop.
- Offer regular opportunities for full body tactile play in different mediums...this will help the overall tactile system learn to process information.
- Another great alternative for affection is to place your cheek firmly against the child's cheek, and move your jaw up and down...see if this is tolerated better than a kiss.
- Regular doses of deep pressure touch to the head and the face can be helpful for tactile processing.
- Offer a vibrating toy or pillow if tolerated well.
- Offer a vibrating oral sensory tool if tolerated well.
- Try kissing the back of the baby's hand to help the baby's nervous system learn to accept this form of affection.
- If you simply can't resist the kiss on the face, make it a firm kiss. Deep pressure tactile input is almost always tolerated better than light touch.

Has to Be Held to Fall Asleep

Sensory Explanation: An infant who struggles with neurobehavioral organization and state transition will probably have difficulty falling asleep independently. This all falls under the umbrella of self-regulation. You are likely providing one or more types of sensory input when you hold your baby to fall asleep...perhaps it is the gentle movement of rocking, or maybe the deep pressure touch and proprioception when holding tightly and cuddling, or the familiar smells from your body and the comforting sound of your voice singing or quietly talking to your baby.

Ideas to Help!

- Try a suspended baby hammock for the gentle vestibular input along with the full body deep pressure touch to support self-regulation.
- Try gentle swinging in a blanket prior to naps and bedtime.
- Try a vibrating crib mattress or vibrating mat.
- Try white noise or soft instrumental music.
- Provide full body deep pressure touch prior to sleep.
- Try compression clothing or snug fitting pajamas.
- Use an essential oil diffuser in the room with calming oils such as lavender.

Flushing of Cheeks

Sensory Explanation: Flushing of the cheeks can be a systemic sign of sensory overload or difficulty with sensory modulation. This is particularly an issue and common trigger from excessive vestibular input from too many directions of movement at one time or for too long. It is also important to consider other triggers such as a food allergy or environmental allergy such as laundry detergent or soaps, including those that the baby comes in contact with from being held.

Ideas to Help!

- Play close attention to flushing of the cheeks when your little one is engaged in a new sensory activity, especially those involving movement.
- Stop a sensory activity immediately of you notice flushing of the cheeks triggered from the activity.
- Flushing of the cheeks can also indicate a fever, and a low grade fever can also be a sign of sensory overload.
- Only use organic and all natural laundry detergents and soaps for yourself and your baby.
- Avoid wearing perfume or fragrant lotions.
- Rule out food allergy possibilities…this can include breast milk. Also, if formula is used, only use non-GMO and organic varieties.
- Full body deep pressure touch may be helpful.

Enjoys Repetitive Play

Sensory Explanation: Repetitive play is very typical and a necessary component of development for an infant and toddler. It is how the brain learns and develops pathways …these pathways are called engrams. It is how the brain remembers something. Repetitive play is also a technique to self-regulate and soothe the nervous system.

Ideas to Help!

- Allow repetitive play as much as needed for this stage in development.
- If it does seem to become difficult to transition the little one to something different, provide a dose of sensory input for the vestibular or proprioceptive system, such as bouncing, or inverting the head, or bear bugs and cuddles while transitioning to a different activity.
- Take note of the times that repetitive play occurs if you feel it has become excessive. Does it appear to be a sensory strategy and coping mechanism to regulate within the environment? If so, decrease the amount of sensory input overall.

Dislikes Hair Washing and Water Poured Over the Head

Sensory Explanation: Washing the hair and head for a baby involves a great deal of tactile input in the form or light and deep pressure touch to the scalp, face, and ears. If the tactile system is over-registering information, this can be uncomfortable and even painful for the baby. The other factor that needs to be considered is the position of the head. It may be the vestibular component and change in position that is not tolerated rather than the tactile input. Two other sensory components to consider would be the smell of the shampoo and also the temperature of the water. Temperature is also processed with the tactile system.

Ideas to Help!

- **Try using a bathing visor to decrease the amount of unexpected tactile input from the water coming into contact with the face and ears.**
- **Watch closely to see if the little one is resistant to the position of the head. Keeping it slightly elevated will likely be tolerated best. If the infant is old enough to sit independently, try hair washing this way instead.**
- **Use organic and all natural shampoo, preferably unscented to eliminate that sensory factor.**
- **Use deep pressure touch to perform the hair washing, and refrain from trying to do it really fast to get it over with. Doing this creates too much sensory input from the tactile and vestibular systems.**
- **Take note of the preferred temperature for the baby, and take the time and effort to achieve this same temperature of water for each hair washing.**
- **On a regular basis provide deep pressure touch to the scalp and head, not just during hair washing…this will help the tactile receptors process information and tolerate hair washing.**

Loves to Be Naked

Sensory Explanation: This is how your baby came into the world and possibly finds it to be the most comfortable. It also provides a unique sensory experience for the tactile system, and it can be a sensory signal to you that the tactile system is having difficulty processing the different textures of clothing. Various clothing textures constantly shifting on the body can be very uncomfortable and even painful for the little one.

Ideas to Help!

- Allow for "no clothing time" at home…or shall we call it "diaper time"? ☺
- Compression clothing can be helpful and worn under clothing.
- Stick to soft cotton, organic clothing when possible.
- Provide regular doses of full body deep pressure touch.
- Encourage full body tactile play in various mediums, especially messy play.

Holds Arms Up and Twists Hands in Circles

Sensory Explanation: This sensory signal is quite common for young infants. This is when the brain and body are learning to coordinate and develop body awareness of the arms and hands, motor planning and motor control. If this continues beyond the developmental phase it may be a sensory anchor and technique used to help self-regulate, calm, and soothe. When a baby does this it provides proprioceptive input to the arms and hands, which tends to be calming and regulating for the nervous system.

Ideas to Help!

- If this movement seems involuntary and persists outside of the times listed above, an evaluation by an OT or PT is recommended.
- Provide deep pressure touch to the arms and hands.
- Encourage weight bearing on the arms and hands, such as over a small therapy ball or tummy time on the floor.
- Provide toys that encourage squeezing, gripping, and banging.
- Utilize other sensory strategies to help calm and regulate such as swinging in a blanket or cuddle swing, bouncing, etc.
- If the little one is developmentally ready, assist him/her in gripping and hanging from a low bar or from your hands.

Shakes or Rolls Head

Sensory Explanation: Shaking the head provides vestibular input for the nervous system as well as a unique visual experience. An infant may be doing this for one or both of these reasons. It can be a way to self-regulate, and the visual and vestibular input simply feels good, or also a way to avoid sensory overload. If your baby does this primarily while in a stationary position, it is likely to increase the amount of vestibular input.

Ideas to Help!

- Limit the amount of time that the baby spends in stationary seats, carriers, and toys, and instead replace with more active, exploratory floor time.
- Increase the amount of vestibular input during the day via swinging, bouncing, rolling, etc.
- Try using a vibrating pillow or other vibrating toy.
- Gently invert the baby's head, supporting at the neck and shoulders. This is best achieved while you are seated and you invert over your lap.
- Go for frequent stroller or wagon rides, making it exciting with lots of curves and bumps along the way.
- If the tot seems to be doing this during times of sensory overload or loud, chaotic multi-sensory situations…decrease the sensory input and find a calm and quiet place to recover.

Does Not Seem to Get Hungry or Eats Way Too Much or Too Quickly

Sensory Explanation: The ability to know when one is hungry or full relies on the sensory feedback to the brain from the stomach. This sensory feedback is from the interoceptors in the gut. If the infant under-registers sensory information, it is possible that sensory information from the gut is also under-registered. This can result in not being able to detect when he/she is full, or on the other hand, may not have much of an appetite.

Ideas to Help!

- Maintain a regular feeding schedule for those nursing and bottle feeding.
- For the self-feeders, help them pace. Often the little ones who eat too much also eat in a sensory-seeking fashion.
- Feed in small portions and small bites, allowing second servings if needed.
- For those who don't get hungry, active floor time play and movement based play prior to mealtime can be helpful.
- Frequent and daily doses of input via the power sensations are very important to improve overall sensory registration. This includes vestibular, proprioceptive, and tactile input.
- Use a vibrating pillow prior to mealtime and also a vibrating oral sensory tool.

Gets Sick or Nauseous After Swinging

Sensory Explanation: Swinging involves a very powerful dose of vestibular input. Babies who struggle with vestibular defensiveness or sensory modulation can quickly and without warning become sick or nauseous after swinging. This can be even more likely when there are quick changes in direction or frequent starts and stops of the swing.

Ideas to Help!

- Watch closely for any signs of distress while swinging. Even a change in facial expression may be your only warning. Other signs to watch for include flushing of the skin or eyes glazing over.
- Tolerating movement is critical for all aspects of development, so an evaluation by a sensory integration OT is strongly recommended.
- Begin swinging in very small doses, as even one minute is powerful. Also, begin in one plane of movement with very little motion of the swing.
- Prior to swinging, have the little one engage in active floor time play.
- Provide a dose of full body deep pressure touch prior to swinging.
- The use of an oral sensory tool while swinging can be helpful.
- The use of a cuddle/lycra type swing or swinging in a blanket is a great way to provide calming and regulating deep pressure touch as well as vestibular stimulation.
- Encourage the body position of full body flexion while swinging.

Frequent Spitting Up

Sensory Explanation: Once medical reasons are ruled out such as reflux and/or a food intolerance or allergy, it is possible that the spitting up can be a systemic response to sensory overload. This can be triggered from one or more forms of sensory input, but vestibular input would be the most likely trigger.

Ideas to Help!

- Rule out medical reasons and/or food allergies or intolerance first.
- Limit the amount of movement following feeding or a meal for at least 1 hour. Even quick changes in position can trigger a vestibular system response.
- After a meal or feeding, elevate the head and upper body slightly if it is nap time or night time and the baby will be lying down.
- Use a Boppy® pillow during bottle or breast feeding to help elevate the head/neck slightly and to encourage slight head and neck flexion.
- If the spitting up seems outside of the normal feeding time range…assess for sensory triggers such as too much movement or multi-sensory input from too much sound, light, and/or touch.

Licks Everything, Including People and Objects

Sensory Explanation: A baby who licks everything is likely doing this to assist in self-regulation and also as a way to identify and explore within the environment. Oral sensory seeking and exploration is the most primitive sense used in utero and during infancy. It plays a very important role in overall development, especially oral sensory processing.

Ideas to Help!

- It's ok, let 'em do it . . . within reason . . . knowing it is part of oral sensory development.
- Offer an oral sensory tool as an alternative, making sure it is available at all times for the child (preferably attached to the infant's clothing).
- Provide regular and daily doses of vestibular and proprioceptive input to help with overall self-regulation.
- Increase the amount of full body tactile play with different textures, from dry to messy. The oral sensory system is also part of the tactile system.
- Olfactory input may also help in this case, and essential oils may help soothe and regulate. Try using a diffuser in the room or a couple of drops of an essential oil on a favorite blanket or soft fabric toy.

Bites Self or Others

Sensory Explanation: The act of biting provides proprioception to the jaw and tactile input to the mouth. This provides oral sensory input, which is likely soothing and regulating for the brain. When the baby bites him/herself, this can be due to sensory under-registration, and it does not feel as painful to the little one as you might think. The act of biting can also simply be a way to achieve a calming form of sensory input that feels good to the nervous system.

Ideas to Help!

- Offer an oral sensory tool...one that offers a decent amount of "bounce" to it and also one that can reach the jaw and molar area. The Ark Grabber® would be my first choice.
- Offer chewy and crunchy foods frequently if the little one is at this stage of oral motor development.
- Encourage drinking pudding, yogurt, or applesauce through a straw if the skill is developed.
- Offer a toddler size Camelbak® water bottle if this skill is developed.
- Try a vibrating oral sensory tool or Z-Vibe®.
- Take note of when this happens the most...is it during challenging situations or sensory overload? Respond accordingly with the use of tools for defensiveness or changing the environment.
- Provide deep pressure touch to the cheeks and jaw line frequently throughout the day.
- Offer frequent doses of proprioception and full body deep pressure touch through play and interaction with the baby.

Sleeps Between Crib Mattress and Edge of Crib, Craves Tight Spaces

Sensory Explanation: The sleep/wake cycle is directly linked to the ability to self-regulate and neurobehavioral organization for an infant. Those who struggle with these areas tend to have difficulty falling asleep and staying asleep. A baby who likes to squeeze into tight spaces to sleep and to just hang out is likely seeking deep pressure touch and proprioception to help with self-regulation and neurobehavioral organization.

Ideas to Help!

- Try using snug fitting pajamas to increase the amount of deep pressure touch to the body.
- Try a vibrating crib mattress or pillow.
- Try a suspended baby hammock.
- Use a squish box or memory foam beanbag with supervision throughout the day, not for sleeping though.
- Provide full body deep pressure touch prior to bedtime and naps.
- Increase the amount of swaddling and use a soft sling baby carrier often.

Refuses to Touch Grass or Sand

Sensory Explanation: Grass and sand are two textures that provide a unique and often uncomfortable type of light touch and tactile input. The other factor is that often this is first experienced when the parent sets the child down on the grass or sand, exposing areas of the body, such as the back of the legs or feet, that rarely come in contact with the new texture.

Ideas to Help!

- Do not force the activity. Let the little one touch and explore the grass and sand when ready.
- First present the grass or sand situation with the hands only, as the hands have been exposed to the most textures and tactile experiences. Do this by having the child sit on the edge of a blanket in the grass or sand, letting him/her engage with the hands when ready.
- For the first experience, keep the rest of the body covered, including socks and shoes, with only the hands being exposed.
- Provide regular daily opportunities for other types of tactile based play from dry to messy.
- Encourage full body tactile play with textures that the tot really enjoys.

Approaches Play or New Textures with Closed Fists or Withdraws Hands

Sensory Explanation: The hands have an enormous amount of tactile receptors, especially the palms; therefore, approaching play or a new tactile experience with a closed fist decreases the amount of tactile input. Also, the first line of defense for the tactile system is to withdraw and not engage in a possibly painful or uncomfortable sensory situation. Just about every situation for an infant is a new experience for the nervous system, and if the tactile system is over-registering information and is sensitive, the brain and nervous system approaches new things "on guard".

Ideas to Help!

- Do not force the baby to touch something . . . ever.
- Provide deep pressure touch to the hands and fingers on a regular basis and prior to new texture related activities.
- Place messy/wet textures in a plastic bag for the infant to explore first...direct supervision is essential for safety using the bag.
- Encourage various types of textures in play, both messy and dry, offering tools such as a shovel or paintbrush. Using a tool first for exploration will help the nervous system become more comfortable with the tactile experience.
- Provide manipulative type toys in various textures...try to stay away from all of the plastic toys. Instead provide toys made of natural materials.
- Encourage exploration of different natural textures outdoors.

Avoids Eye Contact or Shifts Gaze

Sensory Explanation: Eye contact is often misunderstood. When a baby is unable to or has a difficult time making eye contact, it is often a sign of overstimulation or dysregulation of the nervous system. The baby is actually unable to make the eye contact, as it is too overwhelming to the visual system in everyday situations. Eye contact, shifting gaze, and fleeting eye contact are related to neurobehavioral organization and state regulation. It can be particularly difficult for premature infants struggling with over-registration and sensitivity to multi-sensory input, visual input, and social interaction.

Ideas to Help!

- Use this sensory signal as a gauge for how regulated the baby may be at any given moment. It is likely that you will see an increase in eye contact when the infant is in an organized and regulated state.
- During times of lack of eye contact, shifting gaze, or fleeting eye contact, increase the amount of deep pressure touch via swaddling and positioning the infant in full body flexion.
- Decrease the amount of auditory and visual input at that time, as well.
- Gentle, rhythmic swinging in a cuddle/lycra swing, baby hammock, or blanket is also an effective way to promote self-regulation and neurobehavioral organization.
- Take note of your proximity to the infant's face…back off somewhat to see if the eye contact increases.

Gags with Textured Foods, Picky Eater, Extreme Food Preferences

Sensory Explanation: The oral sensory system is a multi-sensory system including tactile, olfactory, gustatory, and even visual and auditory….and if one or more systems is over-responsive, it can make eating an unpleasant experience. The gag reflex is a separate neurological entity, yet is triggered by one or all of the sensory components listed and can be hyperactive and over-responsive. The picky eating and extreme food preferences can be from any of the above sensory explanations.

Ideas to Help!

- Explore various textures, from dry to messy, with hands, feet, and full body on a regular basis to help the tactile system process information.
- Do not force the issue with the disliked food item. Let the baby explore the food with the hands or a utensil on his/her own terms.
- Respect the need for a very specific temperature of food.
- Encourage the use of various oral sensory tools prior to eating and throughout the day to prepare and help the oral sensory system process.
- Use a vibrating oral sensory tool, Z-Vibe®, or vibrating teething toy on a regular basis.

Nail Trimming Distress

Sensory Explanation: The fingertips and fingernail beds are part of the tactile system and have a large number of tactile receptors present. For infants the tactile system is still maturing and learning to process new tactile experiences like this. The fact that this task requires being held in place and very close proximity to others can also contribute to the distress.

Ideas to Help!

- Provide deep pressure touch to hands and feet prior to nail trimming and on a regular basis.
- Sing songs and/or provide a visual distraction or small fidget toy to be held in one hand while the other is being trimmed.
- Try a calm and soothing place for the task, such as having the little one sit in a squish box or cozy on a memory foam beanbag.
- Decrease the other forms of input that may be overwhelming, such as too much background noise or too much light.
- If you have a heavy sleeper…you are in luck…trim the little one's nails while she is sleeping.
- You could also try trimming the nails while the infant is nursing or bottle feeding…but only if this distraction does not cause difficulty with the coordination of suck/swallow/breathe.

Messy Play Is Distressing and Avoided, Including at Mealtime

Sensory Explanation: This can be due to sensory defensiveness and one or more over-responsive sensory systems...including the tactile, oral sensory, olfactory, and/or visual systems. Messy play, especially at mealtime is a multi-sensory experience. The tactile system is the most likely trigger for the avoidance.

Ideas to Help!

- **Offer regular and daily opportunities for messy play. Let the little one initiate the exploration, but always have a wet towel ready to quickly remove the texture from the baby's hands when distressed. Wipe the hands with firm deep pressure.**
- **Encourage crawling over various surfaces and textures, indoors and outdoors.**
- **Offer messy play activities during bath time, so that the tot can quickly get the texture off the hands or body with the water.**
- Move from dry textures to wet/messy textures when offering tactile based play and exploration. This is the natural progression for the tactile system.
- **Offer vibrating toys to help the tactile system process information.**
- Provide deep pressure touch to the hands prior to a tactile activity.
- Never force a child to engage in messy play and resist the temptation to force their little hands in it for even for a second. That one second is enough to cause a systemic reaction (such as nausea) and to trigger fight or flight. The brain will then remember this negative experience and put up a guard to protect the nervous system from future experiences.

Hiccups Frequently

Sensory Explanation: Hiccups can be caused from crying, laughing, or drinking/eating too fast, but hiccups can also be a neurological sign of sensory overload and dysregulation. Pay close attention to the situation, surroundings, and activities that occur immediately prior to the hiccups.

Ideas to Help!

- Remove the baby from the current environment and move to a calm, dark, quiet place.
- Swaddle or use a soft sling carrier for the deep pressure.
- Provide full body deep pressure touch.
- Provide a pillow cave or squish box with supervision and encourage the position of full body flexion.
- Try gentle rhythmic swinging in a hammock, cuddle swing, or blanket.
- Invert the baby's head slightly, supporting the neck, head, and shoulders, then return to upright slowly.
- Provide an oral sensory tool or pacifier.

Resists Movement Such as Swinging, Bouncing, Rocking

Sensory Explanation: This is most likely a sign that the vestibular system is over-responding to input with one or more of the three vestibular canals. This can also be triggered by an over-responsive visual system. Processing of vestibular input is the most important foundational sensory system that impacts almost every aspect of development.

Ideas to Help!

- An evaluation by a sensory integration specialist is strongly recommended.
- Do not force movement, always respect the signal to stop.
- Very small doses of movement are beneficial to the brain…even very gentle and slow rocking is a great place to start.
- Begin with vertical (bouncing) type movement, as this is the most tolerated plane of movement for most infants. Do this in very tiny doses.
- Prior to a movement activity, begin with 5-10 minutes of full body deep pressure touch, swaddling, or positioning in full body flexion.
- Encourage a whole lot of tummy time, rolling, and floor time exploration.
- When handling and holding the infant, be very aware that the quick changes in position may be uncomfortable for one who has difficulty processing movement. Change body position slowly with support of the head and firm pressure touch to the body.
- When working on new linear planes of movement, incorporate full body deep pressure when possible, such as swinging the child in a blanket or using a cuddle or hammock swing.
- Offer an oral sensory tool when working on swinging or new forms of movement.

Touches Objects Very Lightly

Sensory Explanation: This can be explained by an over-responsive and underdeveloped tactile system, with the nervous system being on guard and cautious when touching various textures, especially when the object is new and unfamiliar. On the other hand, lack of proprioceptive feedback and body awareness may be the reason. In this case, the infant is unable to gauge the amount of pressure used in exploring or touching an object.

Ideas to Help!

- Begin by having the infant explore dry textures, working up to tolerating messy textures. Never force a tactile activity.
- Vibration to the hands using a small vibrating toy can be effective in helping the tactile system process information…only do this if the baby is comfortable with it.
- Provide regular and frequent deep pressure touch to the hands and fingers.
- Encourage the use of toys that require banging.
- Encourage manipulative type toys that require squeezing and pinching.
- Encourage a whole lot of floor time play, including crawling over different surfaces.

Does Not Mouth Objects

Sensory Explanation: Mouthing toys and objects is an important part of infant development and the ability to self-regulate. It is also how a baby explores and identifies within the environment. A baby that does not do this is likely showing signs of oral sensory and tactile defensiveness and difficulty processing oral sensory input.

Ideas to Help!

- Provide various textured oral sensory tools, as one may be accepted over another.
- Encourage texture based play for the hands and feet. Begin with dry textures and move up to messy textures…this addresses the overall tactile system in learning to process information.
- Encourage the use of basic musical instruments such as a harmonica or little horn.
- Offer a vibrating oral sensory tool or vibrating teether. Sometimes vibration is tolerated and accepted differently by the mouth.
- Provide regular and ongoing daily doses of deep pressure touch to the face and cheeks.
- An evaluation by a sensory integration OT is recommended.

Hair Brushing Distress

Sensory Explanation: The scalp has a large number of tactile receptors. An infant's tactile system is still developing and may have difficulty with hair brushing due to the large number of sensory receptors on the scalp, and this can be a pretty overwhelming sensory experience.

Ideas to Help!

- Start with a very soft-bristled brush and work your way up to a medium or firm-bristled brush if needed.
- Provide deep pressure touch to the head prior to hair brushing.
- Respect the fact that there can be true pain involved and do not just power through it.
- Sing songs or play soft instrumental music during hair brushing.
- Use essential oils for a de-tangler and for calming olfactory input.
- Offer an oral sensory tool, bottle, or pacifier during hair brushing to help with self-regulation.
- Try having the infant sit in a squish box or in a cozy cuddle swing or hammock during the activity.
- Minimize other forms of sensory input during the brushing…try doing this in a calm, quiet, dimly lit room instead of the loud, bright, echo filled bathroom.

Prefers to "W" Sit

Sensory Explanation: W-sitting is when one sits on the floor with the legs forming a "W" rather than side sitting, tailor sitting, or simply both legs out in front in some way. W-sitting is strongly discouraged as it can cause problems for the hip and knee joints. It also doesn't require crossing midline and trunk rotation, which are crucial for brain development. Often when a baby W-sits he/she is seeking proprioception to the lower body or has poor trunk or pelvic stability.

Ideas to Help!

- Encourage side sitting, "crisscross applesauce", lying on tummy, or long leg sitting instead of W-sitting…depending on the stage of motor development.
- Break this habit as soon as possible! If you nip this one in the bud early, it is so much easier to correct! Just manually assist the change of position by moving the legs out in front.
- Encourage floor time and tummy time play. Rolling, crawling, scooting, etc., all help develop trunk and pelvic stability.
- Offer frequent and daily vestibular activities which require trunk control, such as using a therapy ball or peanut ball for interactive play, or a Rody when the little one is developmentally ready. A platform swing is also a great tool.
- When cueing the little one to switch from W-sitting, keep it fun and playful and offer tactile cues and assistance to switch positions.

Dislikes Being Outside

Sensory Explanation: Being outdoors can be difficult for an infant, especially those who over-register sensory input and have some type of sensory defensiveness. The outdoors is a multi-sensory experience. Being outdoors may be too bright or the unpredictable effects of wind, rain, and loud random sounds (such as a car alarm or a siren) can be overwhelming. Tactile defensiveness could also come into play if the little one is wearing open-toed shoes or has a difficult time with textures to the hands and feet. Outdoor smells can also be a factor. There are many new and unfamiliar smells found outdoors which may be uncomfortable and overwhelming, such as car exhaust, road construction work, smoke, etc. Even pine trees and other fragrant trees and plants can trigger sensory overload.

Ideas to Help!

- Use tools for defensiveness as appropriate. If it is too bright, try sunglasses or a floppy hat. If sound is a factor, use noise cancelling headphones.
- Begin your outdoor experiences in a nice, calm and quiet place in the shade.
- Start by using a soft sling carrier when outdoors to help soothe and regulate the nervous system with the deep pressure touch and proprioception.
- Try using a jogging stroller or wagon for your adventures outdoors.
- An oral sensory tool could be helpful when outdoors to help with self-regulation.
- It's a good idea to bring along a fidget toy or other comfort item when exploring outdoors.

Very Difficult to Calm

Sensory Explanation: The ability to self-calm begins in the womb and continues throughout life. It is quite common for an infant to require assistance in this area as the nervous system matures and develops in the early months of life. This is particularly a challenge for premature babies. The ability to self-regulate relies on an adequate amount of sensory input via vestibular, proprioceptive, and the tactile systems. If the nervous system is having difficulty processing sensory information, the ability to self-regulate is very likely affected…and this includes being able to self-calm.

Ideas to Help!

- Provide an oral sensory tool on a regular basis, including the trial of a vibrating oral sensory tool.
- Swaddle in full body flexion or use a soft sling baby carrier during times of distress.
- Provide a vibrating pillow or vibrating crib mattress.
- Decrease the amount of overall sensory input, particularly auditory and visual.
- Try soft instrumental music or white noise.
- Try an essential oil diffuser with calming oils.
- Provide full body deep pressure touch.
- Do not talk or make sounds at all when the baby is trying to calm down.
- Provide a cuddle/lycra swing or hammock swing, moving in a slow, rhythmic motion.
- Take note of when this happens the most. Is it in social situations? Multi-sensory input environments? Adjust accordingly.
- Provide regular and daily opportunities for input from the power sensations to improve self-regulation and overall sensory processing and nervous system maturation.

Dislikes Wearing Shoes and/or Socks

Sensory Explanation: This is very common for most babies, sensory challenges or not, but there may be a sensory explanation for it as well. If the little one struggles with tactile defensiveness and over-registers tactile input, this could be the reason for disliking shoes and socks.

Ideas to Help!

- Letting a baby go barefoot is actually very beneficial for a number of reasons. It gives proprioceptive feedback to the feet and allows for experiencing new texture.
- When shoes and socks are necessary, take the extra time to make sure the socks are on just right and that the shoes are nice and snug.
- Try seamless socks and also very snug fitting socks for the deep pressure touch.
- Snug-fitting shoes are usually tolerated best since they provide proprioception and deep pressure touch and can dampen the tactile system receptors.
- Provide regular and frequent doses of deep pressure touch to the feet.
- Encourage tactile play involving the feet, in various mediums, from dry to messy.
- To eliminate the taking off of shoes and socks in the car, bring the shoes and socks with you and complete this task right before it is time to get out of the car.

Loves to Look at Spinning or Shiny Objects

Sensory Explanation: Looking at spinning or shiny objects is very common and typical for infants, as it is how the visual system is learning to process information and develop. Looking at spinning and shiny objects can also be organizing, regulating, soothing, and calming for an infant.

Ideas to Help!

- It's ok, let 'em do it…it is part of infant development and is supporting visual processing development.
- Take note of this sensory cue, letting you know that the little one may need support in self-regulation if this happens excessively. Support this by increasing the amount of vestibular and proprioceptive input during the day.
- Limit screen time, preferably not at all until the age of 3 years old. This is not an effective way to support the young visual system.
- Encourage other types of visual based activities which are more engaging, such as toys that require tracking a ball.

Smashes and Grinds Face into Stuffed Animals or Soft Objects (Usually Mouth Open)

Sensory Explanation: This provides deep pressure touch and proprioceptive input to the face and mouth. If the baby likes to do this with the mouth open, it provides additional oral sensory input. This type of activity is often calming for the nervous system and may help the infant soothe and self-regulate.

Ideas to Help!

- Let 'em do it . . . no problem here. Just use this as a sensory signal to provide additional tactile and proprioceptive input and other activities to help self-regulate.
- Full body deep pressure touch could be helpful, as well as deep pressure touch to the face.
- Encourage the use of a squish box, hammock/lycra swing, or memory foam beanbag full of soft pillows and stuffed animals. Direct supervision is required.
- Try a vibrating pillow or vibrating oral sensory tool.
- Offer an oral sensory tool or pacifier.

Rubs Head Along Floor (Bull Dozing)

Sensory Explanation: A baby will often do this in the crawling position. Rubbing the head along the floor while crawling provides proprioceptive input to the head as well as deep pressure touch. There may also be a visual component involved which may be soothing and comforting. An infant who does this is most likely using this technique to help self-regulate by organizing and calming the senses.

Ideas to Help!

- Let the little one do it as long as it is not causing harm to the forehead from too much rubbing.
- If the baby does this a lot, a soft protective helmet could be helpful. The helmet itself will also provide a dose of proprioception and deep pressure touch, which may be soothing.
- Provide gentle head compressions by gentle pressure on the top of the head.
- Assist in inverting the head slightly, supporting the neck, head, and shoulders. Return to upright position slowly.
- Provide regular doses of deep pressure touch to the head, face, and shoulders.
- A snug-fitting hat or compression hat may be helpful.

Glazed-Over Look in Eyes

Sensory Explanation: The sensory explanation for this may be that the infant is in a state of sensory overload and neurobehavioral disorganization and simply cannot take in any more input. It may also be related to strictly visual processing with the glazed-over look being a result of too much visual input; however, sensory triggers or multi-sensory input can also be the cause.

Ideas to Help!
- **Be sure to rule out any other medical explanation such as seizure activity or visual deficit. This is particularly of concern for premature babies.**
- **Use this as your sensory signal to make a change within the environment. Decrease overall sensory input, especially visual.**
- **Offer an oral sensory tool.**
- **Try nursing or bottle feeding to help with self-regulation.**
- **Apply full body deep pressure touch and swaddling, or hold the little one in flexion in a soft sling carrier.**
- **Use sensory tools for defensiveness as needed, such as sunglasses or a floppy hat. Noise cancelling headphones may also be helpful to decrease overall input.**
- **Try calming, rhythmical swinging in a hammock, cuddle/lycra swing, or rocking chair.**

Does Not Feel Pain Like Others, Seems to Lack Awareness of Pain

Sensory Explanation: Pain is interpreted by the nervous system via the tactile system and a specific pathway to the brain. If sensory under-registration is present or if there is processing difficulty via the pain and temperature pathway to the brain, the baby may not register or feel pain like others . . . or at all. Underdevelopment of the overall tactile system is common for premature babies.

Ideas to Help!

- Be very aware of this in regard to safety. If you observe a traumatic fall or injury, it is best to have it evaluated even if the baby does not respond to the painful stimuli.
- Educate family and caregivers in regards to this sensory difference and safety concern.
- Provide frequent and daily doses of input via the power sensations to help overall sensory processing.
- Encourage tactile based play in various textures, working from dry textures to messy textures as tolerated.
- Encourage full body messy play.
- Provide a vibrating pillow and vibrating toys to help the tactile system process.

Overheats Very Easily/Poor Temperature Regulation

Sensory Explanation: Temperature is regulated via the tactile system, and if there is difficulty with tactile processing, the temperature gauge and regulator of the body may not be working well either. Temperature and pain are registered via the same pathway in the spinal cord, so it is common to have processing difficulties with pain and temperature.

Ideas to Help!

- When outdoors, have the baby wear a floppy/bucket type hat.
- Be sure that the baby is dressed for the weather with the special temperature needs being addressed.
- Be sure that the baby is wearing breathable clothing in the summer.
- Always have water available for the little one to drink in hot weather.
- Encourage tactile based play, especially full body messy play to help overall tactile processing, along with frequent doses of vestibular and proprioceptive input to support sensory integration.
- Be sure family and caregivers are aware of the difficulty with temperature regulation.
- Watch for flushing of the skin and cheeks in hot or cold weather as your indicator to make an environment change.

Loves to Be Wrapped Tightly in Blankets and Swaddled

Sensory Explanation: Being wrapped tightly in a blanket provides calming, organizing, and regulating deep pressure touch and proprioceptive input. Not only do most infants crave and love this, it is an essential component of sensory integrative development and neurobehavioral organization, especially for those who struggle with self-regulation.

Ideas to Help!

- The more often you wrap and swaddle the better! This is excellent for the nervous system.
- For even more of a sensory benefit, swaddle and wrap in full body flexion.
- Provide full body deep pressure touch on a regular basis.
- Use a soft sling baby carrier often.
- Position the little one in a squish box or memory foam beanbag, with supervision.
- Try gentle rhythmical swinging in a blanket, suspended baby hammock, or lycra/cuddle swing.
- When the child is wrapped in the blanket, provide additional proprioception and deep pressure touch by holding closely to your body with firm, yet gentle pressure.

Hair Pulling on Self

Sensory Explanation: Although this seems painful, it likely is not for a baby who under-registers tactile input and pain. It may even be soothing and comforting. It may be a sensory strategy that the little one has figured out as helpful in self-regulation. It may also be an indicator of discomfort, dysregulation, irritability, etc.

Ideas to Help!

- Be sure to rule out an illness or medical concern which may be causing the hair pulling, such as a headache or ear infection.
- Provide a fidget toy/object for the baby to manipulate.
- Limit the amount of time the baby spends in a stationary carrier or toy, and replace with floor time exploratory play.
- Try a doll or other toy that has hair. It may meet the tactile need the baby is seeking out with the hands.
- Provide full body deep pressure touch throughout the day.
- Try a compression type hat or beanie.
- Try different oral sensory tools to help with self-regulation and during times of dysregulation.
- Provide regular daily doses of deep pressure touch to the head.
- Encourage full body messy play and other texture based play to improve tactile processing.

Scratches Self

Sensory Explanation: Babies will often do this by accident since fine and gross motor coordination and motor planning are in the early stages of development. But if you see this continue past this stage of very young development, the little one may be doing it for the tactile input, especially if the baby under-registers tactile information or pain. It may also be a technique that the baby has learned to help calm and soothe the nervous system.

Ideas to Help!

- Provide a fidget toy/object for hands…one that offers the squeeze and pinch element.
- A vibrating toy can also be very helpful.
- Use compression clothing/snug fitting clothing on areas where he/she tends to scratch.
- For very young infants, use lightweight mittens or clothing that has the hand coverage option.
- Provide deep pressure touch frequently throughout the day to the hands and areas where the body is scratched.
- Increase the amount of swaddling in full body flexion.
- Try an oral sensory tool as an alternative for self-regulation.

Bangs Toys and Objects Excessively and Intensely

Sensory Explanation: Banging toys and objects is a very important step for the brain in infant motor development. This activity not only provides proprioception to the hands, arms, and upper body, but it also provides many developmental and sensory integrative benefits ... body awareness, gross and fine motor control, shoulder stability, visual motor development, self-regulation, bilateral coordination, and crossing the midline. Tots who tend to do this excessively and intensely may be under-registering sensory input and need to do this more often and more intensely to "feel it".

Ideas to Help!

- Put some earplugs in or wear noise cancelling headphones yourself and let 'em bang!
- Use full body deep pressure touch throughout the day.
- Encourage resistive play for the arms, such as push-and-pull activities.
- Encourage upper body weight bearing activities such as: crawling through a resistance tunnel, modified wheelbarrow walking with support at the hips, use a therapy ball or peanut ball.
- Encourage hanging from a low bar or from your hands when developmentally ready.
- Offer other hard/resistive type play that involves grip strength.
- Offer toys that vibrate to increase the amount of sensory input to the arms and hands.

Seeks Vibration to Mouth

Sensory Explanation: Vibration to the mouth activates tactile receptors as well as provides proprioceptive input to the jaw joints. This type of input can be very helpful for self-regulation and for providing additional oral sensory input, which is often calming and organizing for the brain. It is also a very soothing tool for babies who are teething and can help dampen the pain receptors in the gums.

Ideas to Help!

- Let the baby use vibration to the mouth as needed.
- Provide chewy and crunchy foods when developmentally ready.
- Encourage sucking thick liquids or yogurt/pudding through a straw when this skill develops.
- Provide various oral sensory tools, particularly those that offer vibration.
- Provide deep pressure touch to the cheeks and jaw line on a daily basis.
- When the little one develops the skill to blow, offer basic musical instruments such as a little horn or harmonica.
- Encourage blowing bubbles, including bubbles through a straw.

Drools Excessively

Sensory Explanation: Drooling is a very normal part of infant development, and some babies drool more than others. Excessive drooling can be due to lack of muscle tone and/or proprioceptive awareness of the mouth/jaw structures and muscles. It can also be an indicator that the baby is teething or trying to cut a tooth. One other explanation can be that the infant is a serious oral sensory seeker. Seeking out intense oral sensory input will increase the amount of saliva and drooling.

Ideas to Help!

- Provide an oral sensory tool on a regular basis.
- Try a vibrating oral sensory tool as well.
- Encourage resistive blowing activities when developmentally ready.
- Provide chewy and crunchy foods when developmentally ready.
- Encourage sucking thick liquids or yogurt/pudding through a straw.
- Encourage blowing bubbles.
- Provide deep pressure touch to the cheeks and jaw line on a regular basis.

Enjoy the Sensory Journey...

Ready to learn more and live a sensory enriched life?
Take the next step!

ASensoryLife.com

This handbook was written and intended to work hand in hand with **ASensoryLife.com**. Almost every topic you read about will have further information provided on the website. Use the website to support your understanding and application of the techniques discussed in this handbook. On the website you will find pictures, how-to videos, definitions, printable handouts, and links and ideas for specific sensory tools and equipment. Once on the website, utilize the search bar on the home page and simply enter the word or words you would like to learn more about!

22401592R00060

Made in the USA
San Bernardino, CA
04 July 2015